Humorosity
4 stories
by C. D. Moulton

Reality Sucks!
Every once in awhile, life can get to be a pain in the ass.

Why Me, Lord?
Phil Fethers was having a normal – for him – kind of day. Then the egg exploded.
Well, that was, at least, a little different.

"!"

Sort of gay horror/humor

What a Weekend!
Experiences with going to forums and groups on such as Facebook gave me ideas for this one. If you are a member of any of the types of groups where this kind of people are major contributors, perhaps you will see yourself (Hah! Get real!) as others see you. I reserve a few paragraphs here and there to soapbox on issues. It's called artistic license (like anyone could get a license for *that*!) and I don't pretend any different. I try not to lie to myself. I'm not always successful in that endeavor.

Humorosity
4 stories

© 2015 by C. D. Moulton

About the author

CD Moulton has traveled extensively over much of the world both in the music business, where he was a rock guitarist, songwriter and arranger and in an import/export business. He has been everything from a bar owner to auto salvage (junkyard) manager, longshoreman to high steel worker, orchid grower to landscaper, tropical fish farmer to commercial fisherman. He started writing books in 1983 and has published more than 250 books as of January 1, 2015. His most popular books to date are about research with orchids, though much of his science fiction and fantasy work has proven popular. He wrote the CD Grimes, PI series and the Det. Nick Storie series, Clint Faraday series and many other works.

He now resides in Puerto Armuelles, Panamá, where he writes books, plays music with friends, does research with orchids and medicinal plants – and pursues his favorite ways to spend his time: beach bum and roaming the mountain jungles doing his botanical research. He has lately become involved in fighting for the rights of the indigenous people, who are among his closest friends, and in fighting the extreme corruption in the courts and police in Panamá.

He offers the free e-book, *Fading Paradise*, that explains what he has been through because of the corruption.

CD is the discoverer of the Chadam Protocol for curing cancer.

Facebook page Ambrosua peruviana for cancer.

Reality Sucks!
© 2015 by C. D. Moulton

This is a work of fiction. Any resemblances to actual characters or events is purely coincidental.

Every once in awhile, life can get to be a pain in the ass.

Contents

That Did It!

Harrison Horatius Twilterwaller (What a name to be stuck with!) stood on the jetty, looking over Lake Phonihatchoo, his yacht moored across the wharf, thirty feet away, as the magnificent sunset blazed across the sky.

Okay. So his yacht was a twelve foot Bassman with an old five horse Mercury outboard engine that would start a third of the time and the wharf was an old rickety wooden dock and the jetty a sandy spur. The sunset was also rather blah. There may be a slight touch of pink somewhere up there.

He sighed and took a sip of the Chateau Rothschild 1964 ... he swigged down a gulp of Budweiser.

His knockout ex-supermodel wife, came to the door of the hide-away cabin on the low grassy knoll by the lake in her revealing low-cut dining gown to smile brightly at him, love fairly radiating from her deep violet eyes, and say, in her sexiest voice, "I think the staff has outdone themselves with the cuisine tonight! Dinner is served, if you please?"

Madge (nee Pitts, which she was definitely from) came to the door of the old frame house to screech at him that she wasn't calling him to supper anymore. Brenda (his lovely ... get over it ... fat, sloppy, vicious, drudge daughter) had burned the pizza, but it was all they had, so eat it or cornflakes ... again ... and shut the hell up before you start your bitching!

The sun was below the horizon. A cloud of mosquitos descended.

"Get your stupid ass in here right now or I'll lock you

out!" Madge screeched.

He went to the door and started inside. The place looked like it had been hit by a tornado just after the earthquake and mudslide. His two hundred thirty pound daughter in the dirty pink dress was sitting at the table with a large pizza that smelled like burning hair and garlic in front of her.

"You want I should slice it?" Brenda asked. He shook his head.

"Well! Then what? What should I do? Tear off a piece for you? What do you want me to do with it?"

That did it! He finally snapped!

"Shove it up your lazy fat ass!" He felt in his pocket, turned, walked down to the dock, got in the boat, cranked it (for the first time in months, it started with the first yank), and headed out into the lake.

He had his wallet. He didn't want to see anything else from that place again. He had the secret bank account he'd managed to save a little at the time, originally to surprise his wife with actually living their dream life. Then she had the daughter (he was never sure she was actually his. The doctor had already told him he had a very low sperm count and he had almost zero chance of becoming a father) and started getting fat. Ass first, then boobs, then fill in the middle section. She was what he could only describe as "grotesque."

He had married her when things were still pretty good, if not perfect. The economy was okay, he had a good job, he was educated a year past high school, he'd inherited the little farm on the lake. It was picturesque, if not profitable

Then the bottom fell out. He still had dreams for when things got better. He started the bank account to be able to surprise Madge with a dream castle, fine car, designer clothes, jewels ... all of it.

She was never a real beauty, but had a very nice body. She tended to be lazy, but he would make that meaningless when he could hire a maid for her.

Then she ended up pregnant. He'd known since he was sixteen that he didn't have a very good chance of ever becoming a father. His father had been a little weak in the sperm area, but it was still fifty-fifty. He definitely was the spitting image of his father. He was tested. Not likely. Almost a miracle if he ever fathered a child.

Well, she got fat and even lazier. She raised the girl to be a fat lazy slob, deliberately, it seemed at times. Like mother, like daughter.

He was going to demand a DNA test – if he ever saw them again. He had an idea about that, too!

He could hear her screech over the engine noise. "Harry! What the hell do you think you're doing? Get your ass the hell back here right this minute or you'll regret it! I promise you!"

"What I regret is not doing this ten years ago. Make that twenty four years ago!" he mumbled.

He had his ATM card and more than thirty thousand dollars – and a new life, as of that moment!

He ran out of gas about half a mile before Shoreville, but didn't give a damn. He paddled to the little dock by the Lakeside Restaurant and Lounge, tied up, and went to have a dream meal and to book a room for the night in the hotel next door.

He had a beer on the lakeside deck bar and was talking to a tourist who was wailing that he had come here because of the ads and that there was nothing to do! This was a nothing spot on a nothing lake with a lot of nothing to offer!

Just before he went over the edge and smacked the obsequious asshole in the puss, Sam, the bartender, called to say the phone was for him. His wife. "She said to tell you to turn on your goddamned motherfucking phone. Not quite that elegantly."

He took his cellular out of his pocket, saw that it was discharged, turned, and threw it as far out into the lake as he could. He had a pretty good arm. Probably a hundred fifty feet. It hit flat and skipped three times.

"Gimme a shot of Tequila. And another beer."

Sam did a palm slap and poured him a shot of José Cuervo Especial. "On me. How can you live with someone like that?"

"I can't. Not anymore."

The Journey Begins

Harry packed the clothes and stuff he'd just bought into the suitcase, looked into the full-length mirror, and smiled.

He was really not all that bad looking. He'd always taken care of himself, even when he was the only one in the house who did, and was, if no Mr. Universe, fairly well built. His hair was a mite long, but was still a rich mahogany brown. His teeth had always been good. His 42 year old skin was unwrinkled and smooth. It was an even light tan. His deep brown eyes didn't yet need glasses.

All in all, not bad! He actually looked a little elegant, as he'd always dreamed.

He checked out of the hotel, after getting five hundred from the ATM there, and went to the bus station. The girl at the counter asked where he wanted to go. He asked where the next bus leaving went. She said Atlanta, Georgia, but it made stops in several cities. It had plenty of room. An hour and ten minutes.

He got a ticket. He said he might decide to stay somewhere before Atlanta, but that was yet to be seen.

It was three days to Atlanta, which was a long time on the bus, but he really did enjoy it. He'd never seen much of the country and they went through all kinds of places. He talked with the people in the closer seats at times.

The bus stopped for an hour in all the major cities, so he walked around a bit and got to know a little of what a city was like.

Face it! Shoreville was a little hick town compared to anything like he was seeing now! He'd seen pictures of all of it on the news or in magazines, but they didn't match the reality.

Well, reality, so far as he was concerned, was a load of shit. His life ... the dream part ... was great. Reality sucked.

He saw a ring in a store window. It was platinum with a diamond set in onyx. Six hundred bucks. He bought it.

Atlanta was too much. It was all so impersonal and dirty. And noisy. Everyone seemed suspicious of everyone else. Way too many police. The nightly news, while he was preparing to go to a restaurant, was an hour of crime and violence reports. It was just plain sickening. Then half an hour of national news that was a lot like back ... not home! Not any more! What a great job Obama was doing on one station, what a no-good traitorous bum he was on another. Election year coming up, so a lot of negative crap. We have to get stronger anti-terrorist laws! We have to get rid of those unconstitutional national security laws! We have to get guns out of the hands of the public! We have to follow the constitution and make all guns legal! Gays should have the right to marry! Gays should be stoned to death!

Not one of them was anywhere near the truth about anything. It was all BS from a certain political perspective.

He did know one thing. Atlanta was *not* a place he wanted to stay.

A very attractive woman saw him sitting at the bar, having a beer, and came to sit next to him. She said her name was Miki. He seemed far too handsome a man to be there alone. Was he waiting for some lucky girl or was he married?

He bought her a champagne cocktail and chatted. He said

he'd never been anywhere anything like Atlanta. He didn't much like it. He wanted a place to stay where people were more friendly and there was less crime and noise.

She was getting a bit too close. She put her hand on his leg and said she didn't have much to do tonight, and she was also looking for someone who was more friendly than so many here were.

He was feeling lucky that any woman as good-looking as her, so much younger – she couldn't be over twenty three or four – was attracted to him. Maybe he should have run away years ago! Maybe he could actually finally have his dreams!

A big black man in a purple (!) suit came to say Mr. Norman had tonight. Don't try to do any side jobs or she'd learn just how smart that act was, bitch! He told Harry he had several other girls who weren't booked for tonight. Two fifty for two hours. Miki was looking disgusted.

She was a prostitute! Reality sucks.

He told the black, "I don't think any of them are worth a dollar and a quarter an hour."

The bartender was right there. He laughed and said, "Well, maybe Wanda. Spike, you take your girls outside. You've been warned not to work inside this place."

The black and Miki left. The bartender told Harry to watch his back around that bunch.

He finished the beer and looked around. No one there he wanted to talk to, so he left.

He saw a flash of purple just at the corner, so was ready when he was grabbed by the big black man and pulled toward the alley. He saw that kind of thing on TV a lot, so suddenly moved toward the man, who was surprised enough to try to back away and found his head smashed against the brick wall. He dropped to the pavement and got a shoe in the face, then the mud wiped from the shoe on his fancy purple suit.

Miki was standing there with her hand to her mouth, wide-eyed.

"Now comes the part where you take your little twenty five from your purse and I take it away from you and shove it up your ass and pull the trigger, right?" Harry asked.

She put her hands up and backed away. Harry went on to his hotel. He would try the bar there and go to bed early. He wanted to get out of Atlanta as early in the morning as he could.

Reality sucks.

He always thought that stuff on TV was just movies, but here it was, and he was caught up in it. He was just lucky he and Gene horsed around with those moves they saw on TV until they were both pretty good.

In the morning, he went to the airport to find a place to try. He was headed to Mobile, Alabama, in three hours. He got a newspaper and sat in a restaurant at the airport to wait. The local news was on the TV, listing the crimes of the day. It was all one paragraph stories. A fight in a pool hall, four injured. Suspects in custody. Known mobster Cambierte was being questioned about two gangland murders. A local pimp, Spike Anderson, was found beaten and shot through the heart and robbed of an undetermined amount of cash and more than six thousand dollars worth of gold chains and rings off Apple Street in an alley. (*Bet Miki saw a chance! I'll buy her another champagne if I ever see her again!*) Two teenagers were killed execution style...

It would be damned good to get away from Atlanta!

The ride in the plane was fair. It was his first time, and he was surprised he wasn't a bit more afraid, but he relaxed and enjoyed talking with the Japanese man who owned a small food store in Mobile.

It was drizzling rain when he got off the plane. He got a cab and found a reasonable hotel.

He'd already decided Mobile wasn't going to be the place. North? South? West?

He bought a cell phone, a Blackberry, actually. His daughter spent eight hours a day on a Smart Phone, so he got an idea. He registered on Twitter, which she spent most of her time on, as urxdadthnx2gd and punched a message to lakesirensxy1: tell ur mthr 2 dvrc & tk frm nada ls n no contest. f no, yrs trly dvrc hr w/DNA n u.

He sent it and waited for the answer. Four minutes: *????!!! U gt bck!!! ur crzy!!!!*

He sent: *tk r lv. 1 wk. answr nw*

He waited. He knew her: *bnk acct?*

prt f frm nvr hr frm u agn. deal?

OK

Now for the new life. Florida. South. On gulf. Get a job or start something.

Bradenton, Florida, is a nice little laid-back town. It also had plenty of jobs he was able to handle. He worked for a farm supply depot for three months, which paid the bills plus a little. He rented a large old but solid estate house on a canal off the river a couple of miles out of town when he made a deal with the owner, an old woman who had no heirs she would leave a thin dime to. He would pay the back taxes, because she was about to lose it anyway for that. It was a little over twelve thousand dollars. The property was worth well over a million dollars, and he would get it when she died. She made out a right of survivor title with him as minor stockholder. He wouldn't have to pay taxes when she died.

He then decided to fix it up to its former elegance. It really was well-designed, and it really was elegant, in a Southern Plantation Mansion way. It was structurally a lot stronger and better than modern crap.

He got a job offer from the main supplier to the fertilizer depot. Area representative. Double his present salary and commission plus bonus. Things were looking up! Two days per week going to all the outlets and helping with inventory control. He had the sense to spend a third day one week of the month to go to all the places that didn't buy from the depot to see what the competition was like. He was able to offer most of them good deals with his company on some items to where they would all make out.

He met Louise and Charlie Gordon, from Shoreville, at one of the stores. They knew each other from a year ago, when they moved to Florida. They kept in touch with the people there on the net. They asked about Madge and the daughter. He said they had issues and were divorced. At least, Madge had filed, according to what he knew.

He told him about how much better things were here than in Shoreville. They agreed that things had gone from the bottom up to where they were doing very well since they left. Leaving Shoreville was probably the best decision they had ever made. It was nowhere, on the road to nowhere.

He bought a lot of material to work on his house and

spent the next two days refurbishing some of it. When he went to the office on the third morning there was a legal certified letter waiting for him. It seemed that Madge had, just yesterday, modified the divorce agree-ment. He would have to give her half of everything he had.

It seemed that Louise Gordon had told Eileen Fabers about his good fortune, and that Eileen had told her daughter, Sara, who was a friend of his own daughter on Twitter. Madge had immediately gone to her lawyer.

Reality sucks. Try to be a friend to someone, this is what happens.

He then grinned at the letter and turned on the comp, went to Twitter and sent a PM to lakesirensxy1: *This voids the agreement. Tell Madge that there will be a DNA comparison with you and me. She will then get exactly half of the farm and half of the bank account. The half of the bank account will pay for my half of the farm, so she can get what she had minus the bank account. No shorthand here. I have your DNA chart from the test for genetic disease when you were born. Thank her for me. She can probably sell the place for enough to get by for awhile, but she'll have to lose about a hundred thirty pounds and clean herself up to be able to get a job.*

He sent it. He sat back to wait for the answer. It didn't come before lunch, but was there when he got back. It was from a lawyer. It asked that he call a number in Shoreville to discuss the litigation procedure concerning his wife and daughter.

He sent back that he wasn't about to spend any money calling some hick lawyer who was trying to rip him off.

That got a quick answer!

Mr. Twilterwaller: If you wish to enter into a bitter court battle that you will surely lose, so be it. I merely wished to moderate the difficulties such processes engender. You will receive a summons, should you not cooperate in a civil manner. I am only trying to lessen the negative aspects of such confrontations.

He smirked and replied:

Mr. Thrasher: I would recommend not paying a courier to place a summons from a local court in Missouri into my hands here in Florida, personally, as it would end up with me laughing in his/her face. The most Madge could get was by dropping the case and keeping the farm and bank account. One look at her, along with the DNA charts that prove Brenda is not my daughter and she'll be lucky if the court doesn't say she gets nothing and must vacate the property at once.

Six minutes later:

Mr. Twilterwaller: You have no DNA charts with Brenda Mae Twilterwaller's DNA to test and there will be none taken, so your threat is meaningless. Expect a summons.

He laughed, and sent:

Mr. Thrasher: When Brenda was born the fact that I had possible genetic problems caused Dr. Edinger to ask that we have her genetic records to see if she carried any problematical factors. I was not compared at that time, but the chart was made and I have a copy I gave to Dr. Pendergas for comparison. Guess what?

He didn't expect any fast answer to that. He made up the part where he had a copy, though he could get one very easily from the lab in Templeton, where the test was made. He made up Dr. Pendergas, too, but Thrasher was lying, so that gave him license, the way he saw it.

He went on his route for the afternoon and went out for

a few beers that night. He met a really nice-looking woman, even in her work clothes and with no make-up, about thirty, who he liked. she had a great sense of humor and was open to suggestions of how to spend her time. She didn't mean beddy-bye. That would wait until she knew him and would happen or it wouldn't.

Lorna Kingsley. He arranged to see her Saturday night for a dinner and the live band at the plantation house.

Next day, while he was painting the front of the house, Louise and Charley Gordon drove in and wanted to talk to him. It was about his situation in Shoreville.

"Situation in Shoreville? I don't have any situation in Shoreville anymore."

"Eileen Fabers is my cousin," Louise announced.

"I don't think I remember ... isn't she that dark-haired woman who lives over the ... oh, yeah! Brenda and her daughter are friends or something."

"Eileen called and said that you abandoned Madge and Brenda. You left them destitute! That is hardly the impression you gave us!" Charlie snapped. "The Bible tells us what will happen to people like you."

"I left them with the title to the farm and about eight thousand dollars in the bank. That's hardly destitute."

"But Brenda's at the age she has expenses. She is isolated from her friends. That is not acceptable!" Louise spat.

"Well, number one, twenty two isn't all that expensive a time. She weighs over two hundred pounds at five seven. She is lazy and doesn't bother to keep herself or the place she inhabits clean. She is isolated by her own choice and has no friends because of her personality.

"Number two, it's none of your goddamned business!"

"Here! Here! There's no need for this blasphemy or to let this get out of hand!" Charlie cried. "We are concerned for the welfare of our neighbors back home, particularly family!"

"What the HELL!?? *Family*!?? It has nothing to do with your family!"

"Er, well, um," Charlie replied. "The reality, uh, is that it might – indirectly! – have some, er, concern, if you will, with a member or, er, um."

"Reality sucks. There's no way ... unless ... My god! *you're* the father of Brenda!?"

"EEP! NO!" Louise cried. "You see, my brother is ... his position, you see, and Madge is threatening ... Charlie, we aren't part of this! We should stay away from this type of people!"

"Your brother?"

"Uh, her brother is Reverend Lucas. You can see...."

"*What*? You want me to give that thing I was married to everything I have because your *brother* is a two-bit phony excuse for a trifling preacher! Are you totally insane or just amazingly stupid?!"

"Come on, Louise! I suppose Bubba, here, needs a lesson about life's little realities!" He took a swing at Harry, who ducked and came up to deliver a fast roundhouse to the side of the head. Charlie dropped to his knees. Harry looked at Louise, who was standing there like (a flashback) Miki, with the hand to the mouth and wide-eyed.

"Reality sucks. You two get off of this property or I'll have you arrested. Come back when you can't stay so long.

"Bad idea. Don't come back." He turned and went

inside.

Was he in some kind of space warp or something? This couldn't be happening!

The Gordons drove away. He went out to finish painting. The place really was elegant when it was fixed up. He would restore the original landscaping and put a load of pea gravel on the drive. It would look like 1868, when the place was originally built.

He finished the painting and was putting the supplies away when the sheriff drove in and came to ask if he was H. H. Twilterwaller.

"Uh-huh. What?"

He handed Harry an arrest warrant. For assault and battery, threats and slander.

Harry grinned at the sheriff, who tried to hide a grin, himself. "Gordon? Really?"

"Ain't they a trip? Statement from her took more than an hour and a half. He swore it was true to avoid having to give one, himself. She sort of got carried away, so you can explain why he has a black eye and I'll let it lay until it gets to court, if they don't drop it.

"I'm Carey Hanks, local gendarme."

"Harry. Together we're Harry-Carey.

"Okay. Bad pun, but that's the only kind I know.

"Charlie tried to get me to pay off my ex-wife so it won't come out that Louise's brother, the Right Reverend Lucas, knocked up my wife and I've raised their daughter for the past twenty three years. I said he was insane, at best, to even suggest anything like that. He was going to teach me a lesson. I ducked and smacked him, then told them not to come back here or they'd be arrested."

"He swung at you, first? He said you hit him when he

didn't even expect it for no reason, except that you are an atheist and didn't like for him to say anything from the Bible about what happens to perverts who abuse their own children."

"Did he actually say anything like that BS in a sworn written statement? Really?"

"She did. He swore it was true. It's not the first time she's gone out into oogy-boogy land about someone. She thinks, because they're so rich, she can get away with anything. She'll cause you trouble. They're big shits at the country club and such. They're just pains in the ass for me."

"So. They're rich? Why don't they pay off my ex?"

"I guess they want to keep their names out of it. Who knows?"

"Well, maybe we can bring a little more reality into their lives, huh?"

Palm slap time!

A Little Reality

Things went along a little more tranquilly for awhile. He dated Lorna Kingsley several times. They got along a lot better than just well. She had divorced a cheating, violent husband and he had ditto with ex-wife.

When she dressed up, she was really beautiful. It turned out she used to be a spokeswoman for a home appliance company. She could make the tone of her voice say a lot of things the words didn't.

He finished the outside of the house and had the landscaping looking very authentic for the period. Lorna had a very strong sense of design, where he would just try to copy pictures. He had the entrance to the river dredged out to its original depth and built a good dock. He liked the water and the river went into the bay, then into the gulf. He got a 16' MasterCraft with a sixty five horse Yamaha engine.

He got his first bonus. He thought there was a mistake. fifteen hundred, maybe, with a misplaced period. It actually was fifteen thousand! He was the top salesman in the southeast! He also got a raise of two hundred a week! Merry Christmas!

He traded in the MasterCraft for a 32' HarborCraft.

He bought a BMW, trading in the 4 year old Honda he bought when he moved to Florida. He carried a platinum ATM card!

On the 1st of January, he married Lorna. They decided the perfect place for a honeymoon was right there in what was actually a mansion in paradise to them.

On the 6th of January he got the notice that he was being

sued by the Gordons. He had become friends with Carey. They went fishing together a lot. Carey had a fun wife and a son just ten years old. Carey brought the summons – and a copy of the statement.

"My wife's uncle is a civil lawyer. He's run across Gordon before. He had a suit by him dropped when he could prove the statement was false that led to it. They're so rich they think they can buy off anyone. They spout all that Jesus crap when they're slandering everybody around them."

Harry got in touch with William Hallowell, the lawyer, got an appointment, and took what he had. Carey had told Bill about the statement.

Hallowell read over the pages, an evil grin growing as he turned the pages.

"She slandered about anyone she ever met, didn't she?"

"Well, isn't the fact that it is in a written sworn statement libel, not slander?"

"Uh-huh. And definite deformation. How much should we counter sue for?"

"How much can we get?"

"Twenty five percent?"

"Sounds like a winner!"

"Oh, it's definitely a winner!"

"A million?"

"Fifty million, but we'll settle out of court for thirty. They have insurance, but I think the way she went on will mean they only pay a percent."

"How much will we collect?"

"About twenty six, after expenses and all that."

"I can scrape by on that!"

They shook hands. Harry went home to wait four days

until trial.

"Mrs. Gordon, is it true that you were called to the home of Mr. Twilterwaller to discuss his ex-wife and daughter and to arrange for their welfare, when Mr. Twilterwaller suddenly cursed and attacked your husband because he mentioned the Bible and what...." Bernard Benson, counsel for the plaintiff, asked.

"Objection!" Hallowell yelled. "Isn't the witness supposed to be the one giving testimony here?"

"Just objection will do, counselor. Sustained," Judge Collins replied.

"I was merely laying foundation for the fact that my clients were drawn to a location...."

"One more word of testimony from counsel and I throw your case out!"

"Er. Well, Mrs. Gordon, please tell us what happened, in your own words."

She went into a spiel about how Harry came to their place of business where they were lured to that pervert's place by trickery and lies about how he wanted to provide for his daughter and ex-wife, who he admitted he had shamelessly abandoned and left destitute when he ran to Florida to be with a whore on the streets who ....

Bill had to keep Harry from jumping up and yelling what he thought of anyone who would say that kind of thing.

She finally ran down. Bernard thanked her for her honesty and sincerity and waved as he headed back to the plaintiff's table. She started to get up. Bill said, "Please retain your seat, Mrs. Gordon. I will cross-examine. You leave the witness stand when the judge says you can, not when your lawyer says you can."

Judge Collins rapped her gavel, but grinned slightly. Bill stood and approached the witness stand, reading some pages. He stood in front of her a moment, shook his head, and said, "Let's be clear. You claim that Mr. Twilterwaller came into your place of business and asked that you go to his place to discuss his ex-wife?"

"He claimed that he wanted to try to make things right with her. He abandoned her and his daughter and left them destitute and without any way to even get food! He said he knew that was wrong, that he wanted to make it right! My husband said he would be forgiven by the lord, Jesus Christ, for his act of remorse. That pervert tried to hit my husband, but he left in a few minutes."

"You are saying he came to your place of business, attacked your husband, then you went to his place later?"

"Er."

"Well? Is that what you are saying?"

"Uh, that is, we later, uh, had him say he was sorry, that he had, uh, that is, gone too far."

"I see. That isn't in the sworn statement you gave to the police – but neither was much of anything you claimed a moment ago here.

"Do you know Virginia Willis?"

"Virginia? Yes, She worked for us for a couple of weeks before Christmas."

"In your home or in your place of business?"

"Business. The staff at the house has been the same for more than two years."

"She was working for you at the time Mr. Twilterwaller came to confront you and your husband?"

She looked at Benson in panic and shook her head. Benson made it a point not to be looking at her at the time.

"Mrs. Gordon? Answer the question," Judge Collins ordered.

"I, uh, around that time, possibly, I think."

"She was, in fact, within six feet of you the entire time Mr. Twilterwaller was in your place of business to take notes about the possible future orders. Isn't that true?"

"Er, um."

"I'll take that as a 'Yes.' Perhaps you can explain why she didn't observe the confrontation or hear anything like you claim in your sworn statement? Why the only mention of the ex-wife was that he had gotten a divorce, uncontested by him, as it was sought by her, and that she was provided for by being given the farm and homestead and a sizeable bank account, of which he could have, under Missouri law, claimed fifty percent of? Why she didn't observe any harsh words at any time and definitely no attack or attempted attack?"

"Objection! Badgering the witness!" Benson yelled.

"He asked her about the testimony I will assume is to be proffered by another witness," Judge Collins replied. "Proceed, counselor."

"As your non-answer is more defining than an answer could be, we can move to other parts of your statement. The one you made sitting right there just minutes ago, the statements you made under an oath before the court and God.

"You referred to a whore on the streets, who Mr. Twilterwaller ran away with or some such slanderous nonsense. I had to restrain Mr. Twilterwaller from actually attacking you right here. It was a very difficult thing, as I know his wife and know she is a far more moral and honest person than you can possibly claim to be.

"Is Mrs. Twilterwaller, the present Mrs. Twilterwaller, the one to whom you referred?"

"Er, no. Of course not."

"Then who?"

"I don't know her name. I was told about it by a friend at the church."

"Then who was the friend? We can ask him or her about the statement."

"I don't remember."

"Then we will add slander and deformation of character against you, who repeated that falsification right here in this courtroom, to the countersuit already filed. Your only recourse will then be to produce that person or those persons, who will be added to another suit.

"Now! About your being lured to his home so that he could attack your husband.

"We have shown, by your own testimony, that it was not at the time when he visited your business. He did not know you were in the area, at that time. He met you by surprise when he came into your place of business to discuss business. He mentioned his ex-wife and daughter in passing at that time-

"When and how did he lure you to his home?"

"Er."

"That's hardly an answer."

"I refuse to answer anymore questions! You're trying to trick me!"

"Asking that you substantiate your sworn testimony is trickery?

"Your honor, we have shown this witness, the plaintiff in this case, is a perjurer and can't be believed in any instance having to do with this case. In doing so, we have also proven the countersuit.

"Is it necessary to continue?"

"Plaintiff?"

"We ... might I have a word with my client?"

"Recess fifteen minutes. You and your client will remain in the courtroom and all others will step outside. The jury will leave the room for that time. Do not discuss this case in any way with anyone until verdict is discussed in jury chambers." Judge Collins rapped the gavel and everyone except the Gordons and their lawyer and a representative of the insurance company left the room.

"How could Benson be so stupid as to put her on the stand instead of him?" Bill asked. "What will you do with the thirty mil? I ain't about to lower it after that!"

"Give me twenty cash and you keep the rest for all your trouble."

Lorna came to them to smile brightly. "Why didn't you tell me you were running around with whores before I married you?! I want a divorce! I'll gut and scale you and leave you on the streets!

"After you get the twenty mill, of course."

"I can always pimp my whore girlfriends out and make a living!"

They laughed and joked. The insurance company lawyer came to ask to talk in private with Bill, who winked and moved to the side with the lawyer. Lorna and Harry got sodas from the machine and chatted and teased until the bailiff came to tell them to all come inside again. Bill had gone in already and was in conference with Benson at the bench. Collins was there and nodded, then the bailiff said to take their seats and shut up, but in slightly more genteel words.

Collins called for order, declared court was in session, and said for the plaintiff to proceed.

"Call for mistrial," Benson said.

"Denied, Proceed," from Collins.

"Plaintiff rests."

"Defense?"

"With court's questions, if we might? We wish to make this very embarrassing session to be shortened as much as possible."

"Very well. Plaintiff's case was not proven, based on perjuries committed by the plaintiff. Defense prevails. If there are questions from the jury, to be considered only in seeking proper actions and/or compensations.

"Mrs. Foreman?"

A rather sour-looking middle-aged woman stood. "I don't know what you want. If you mean, do I have any questions, I most certainly have a couple, myself."

"Your questions and those of other people sitting jury," Collins replied.

"Very well. I want to know about the ex-wife and their daughter and what really happened. Did he actually abandon them or did they have an amicable divorce, though I don't believe in divorce, personally. What is their present situation, particularly the daughter?"

"Mr. Twilterwaller?" Collins asked.

"My ex-wife and I had issues since Brenda was born. I didn't approve of the way she was being raised. Madge, my ex-wife, seemed to be deliberately teaching her to be lazy and irresponsible.

"I discovered Brenda is not my daughter, that she is the daughter of a preacher at the local church, which is what the Gordon's confronted me about. The preacher is a relative.

"I left Madge and Brenda the farm, which is valued at about sixty five thousand dollars now, but is rising in value regularly because it's on a large lake. There was about eight thousand in the bank account, which I also gave them.

"Mrs. Gordon got in touch and tried to start trouble because she was afraid it would come out that Brenda was her ... the preacher's daughter, and that I was tricked into supporting her for twenty three years. Even her lawyer agreed that I didn't have to give them anything. I could even have them evicted from the property, but I would never consider anything like that for a single second. They are and will always be a part of my life." Might as well try for a few brownie points with the type. When he said Brenda's father was a preacher, half the jury of four women and two men looked shocked. Bill had told him that, if they got a jury like that, with middle-aged church women, the Gordons were dead in the water if it came out that Harry had been tricked into supporting a child not his own – by a supposed man of God! The "Part of my life" would be a good line to lay on them.

"I am shocked that a ... can you prove ... I don't....

"Mr. Twilters, what about the whores she accused you of consorting with?" She made the "she" almost a curse in itself.

"I am at a loss. I do not believe in ... well, I know there are situations where a girl may be forced ... I don't know what that was about! It is a slander and a lie! I do *not* consort with those poor unfortunate people! (Bill said to knock it off or he'd lose them, just under his breath.)

"I'm sorry. I shouldn't let those kinds of ... I apologize.

That was uncalled for. It is just so humiliating to hear such accusations. I am married to a fine and moral woman. There is no way ... I'm sorry for my outburst."

The woman sat down and looked around. A man stood, and said, "Did you know that the girl was not your daughter?"

"Well, yes and no. I had a doctor's diagnosis that I have a low sperm count and that I could probably never be a father. It was just barely possible. I didn't *know* until Madge's lawyer said there would be no DNA test. If she was my daughter, there is no way *she* wouldn't demand the test. She was over twenty one and was the one to have the say as to that. It tells me she knew I wasn't her father.

"When she was born, there was a genetic trait test because of my own genetic problems, such as the low sperm count. It was simple for (Bill was wide-eyed. Wrong tack!) my lawyer, in Missouri, to get her chart and have it compared, though I kind of wish I'd have never found out the truth."

The man nodded and sat. (Later, Harry learned that the man's brother was caught in a scam by a girl who had a baby she claimed was his. A DNA test proved it wasn't.)

"Anything further?" Collins asked. There wasn't, so she recessed for the jury to deliberate about penalties. Bill took Harry and Lorna to lunch at a good restaurant. "After all, I'm going to make a couple mil off of you, minimum!"

Bill said the insurance lawyer made a deal where the company would pay 80% if the perjury charges were dropped.

"Why?" Lorna asked. "They could refuse to pay any-thing because it was fraud all the way on the part of the Gordons."

"And end up spending five times that in court costs fighting their suits that a jury would award them millions, because it's just a crooked insurance company," Bill explained.

It was surprising that the jury was out only during the lunch hour. They had asked the court only one question, concerning the assets of the Gordons. Bill said that was a little scary.

"Why?" Harry asked.

"They decided the Gordons were attacking Christian values in a case of fraud."

"But why scary?"

"Because that kind of thing means they'll want to send a warning to all the other hypocrites out there that God will take everything they have away. Then we get appeals and end up with the twenty five mil or so after months in courts.

"We end up famous or infamous, depending on point of view, through no fault of our own. I wish you hadn't given that little psychological speech. I *really* wish you hadn't apologized for it."

When they returned, court was just going back into session. Judge Collins asked if the jury had come to a decision. The woman stood.

"Your honor, this is getting altogether too much of a crooked scam, where people try to cause others unknowable misery through no fault of their own.

"Mr. Twilterwaller did no wrong. He, in fact, went a very long way out of his own interests to try to do the right thing in an impossible situation, then that Gordon woman (that was pronounced like she was speaking of the lowest type of slimy garden slug) tries to make money on it by charging him with so many ... it is unacceptable! We read the entire statement she gave to the police, and that her husband (another, even lower slug) swore to the truth of.

"She even called him a *pervert*! There was never any hint of ... it is unacceptable.

"We discovered that this is not the first incident where these two ... persons ... have done these atrocious slanders of innocent people.

"Your honor, we find for the defendant, the plaintiff in the counter suit, one hundred dollars in damages. Additionally, we find in the amount of one hundred million dollars for character assassination and deformation of character!

"We find the assets of these people amount to more than one hundred eleven million dollars, so this will not leave them in the condition in whch they tried to leave Mr. Twilterwaller, though several of us wished to do exactly that!

"That is our decision!"

"So say you all?"

They all agreed.

"Court awards penalties as of the suggestion of the jury. Thank you for your time and consideration. You are excused."

Lorna said, "I want a new yacht!"

"Then get a job and earn it!" Harry shot back. They hugged each other for a very long moment. The woman from the jury smiled sweetly at them. Harry went to take her hand and say she was a wonderful, understanding and caring person, and that she would be blessed.

"I guarantee you that Madge and Brenda will get a share of it. It is not the fault of the girl that her birth ... it is best forgiven and forgotten. I moved on from that. One must not allow such things to fester. I am sure Madge had sought forgiveness in her own way, and that she will receive all the forgiveness she deserves."

"You are a good man. May God bless you forever. I will leave you now, knowing we have done the right thing.

"My dear, you have married a good man. There aren't that many, anymore. You are blessed."

"I know. I thank you so much. It hurt all of us so badly when these awful ... we have to let it go. It's in the past," Lorna replied.

"You are wise, my dear. God bless you!" She walked away with a smile for everyone.

"You people are sickening!" Bill said. "How about we go to the bar and celebrate with a good cold drink and a couple of those whores you are always running around with?

"Are you really going to give your ex and not-daughter anything?"

"What they deserve is all I promised, but I'm such a great guy I'll give them each a hundred grand to get out of my life and stay out. You can write it up so that, if they try anything in the future, they have to return the hundred grand."

"I agree, but it should be maybe a dollar apiece," Lorna suggested.

"Be fair! It should be five dollars apiece!" Bill cried.

"Is this real?" Harry asked.

"We'll know in about ten minutes. Here come Franklin, the insurance lawyer."

The lawyer came up. "Okay. You did it to me. How much?"

"What, Harry? Forty mil for you, ten for me? Franklin, here, expected that from the start."

"I can live with that, I suppose."

They shook hands all around. Franklin said they would pay sixty percent after the Gordons paid the forty.

"What will we do with the ten percent over?" Lorna asked.

"Pay the taxes in an agreement," Franklin replied.

"Is this real?" Harry repeated.

"It's real," Bill said.

Back to Reality

H. H. Twilterwaller laid in the chaise lounge and took a sip of his Haig Scot's Whiskey on ice, flicked a bit of lint off of his smoking jacket (though he didn't smoke) and looked out at the fantastic sunset across the river past his yacht.

He sighed deeply.

Lorna, his knock-out wife, came onto the deck with a tray of nice little aperitifs from several countries. She had on a nice sun dress that showed her exceptional figure well.

"Chateau Briand for dinner. I didn't want to cook anything difficult."

She was a master chef, too! She insisted on cooking for him.

"Want to run down to San Blas for the weekend? I'd like to make a little trip in the new boat. We can come back slow and stop at all the places. Just the two of us. And Freddie (the boat captain).

"Well, Annette. We can't ask Freddie to spend that much time away from his wife, and Annette and I buddy around a lot. We'll have a blast on the islands."

"Okay. Sounds like a plan!"

Sometimes, reality doesn't suck.

Why Me, Lord?
© 2013 by C. D. Moulton

This is a work of fiction. Any resemblances to actual persons (except me) or events is purely coincidental

Phil Fethers was having a normal – for him – kind of day. Then the egg exploded.

Well, that was, at least, a little different.

Contents

Birthday 30

Phil Fethers woke up early with a headache and his right foot hurt.

He groaned. Not another day like yesterday! It simply couldn't go on and on and on and on. It was his birthday, and he woke up to dread, not joy.

Hell, not even contentment.

Phillip James Fethers, 30, as of today.

Why the hell didn't they name him Tarand Fethers? It would fit his life!

He swung his leg to the side. Charlie horse! He screamed a short agonized, "Gheee!" and grabbed for his foot. Pull back on the toes. The charlie horse lessesed. He worked the knee a bit, sighed, swore, and stood. Today would be Hell plus. He should stay in bed.

The way he had to piss, even that would lead to disaster.

He went to the bathroom. This was, at least, something he could get relief from. He took a long piss, stepped back, flushed the toilet – which was clogged, somehow. The water came over the rim and was running onto the floor. The float didn't cut off the fill. He dove for the cut-off valve, banging his head on the sink The flow stopped, but he had a mess.

What's new? He went to the cabinet for the mop. The detergent was turned over and had run onto the floor. He stared at it a few seconds, shook his head, took the mop to dry the bathroom floor, went back, put the mop in the cabinet and took out the plunger.

He didn't ask why the toilet was clogged. There was no answer. He had put nothing in it that could clog, but this kind of thing happened much to frequently to him for him to waste time wondering about it.

He got the toilet to working. He had the water squirt all over him when he used the plunger. He stepped into the shower to rinse off. There was a sudden knot in the arch of his foot. He slipped, but managed to grab the shower curtain before he fell onto the tile.

That pulled part of the rings off the rod, of course.

The phone rang. Why?

He was in the shower. Of course it rang. It always did.

Fuck it! He went into the hall wet to answer the phone. It quit ringing just as he got to it. Naturally.

He went back to the bathroom and towelled off. The phone rang again. He answered it. Jennie Wright. Pain in the ass needy girl who had latched onto him tighter than a leech. He didn't want to hurt her. He didn't want to hurt anyone, so he ended up being hurt. Every time.

There was a party at her place. Seven thirty. It was for him. Be there.

He went to the kitchen, put on the coffee and got out the bacon, eggs and makings of an omelet – which would turn into scrambled eggs with vegetables and bacon bits before he was done. He never could turn an omelet.

He dumped the mix into the hot skillet. A bit of hot oil spattered on him. A couple of burn blisters. Small, for a change.

There was a knock on the front door. Crap! It was too early for anyone he knew to be here!

He turned the stove off and went to the door. Four Jehova's Witnesses or Seventh Day Adventists or something were there. Two men and two women. He opened the door. They were shocked. The women squealed and ran down the walk. The men stared a second, then said they didn't need any perverts in their church and marched off.

Shit! He forgot he got out of the shower and went directly to the kitchen. He didn't put anything on.

Maybe that would work out alright. That bunch definitely wouldn't return!

Wrong! He went back to the kitchen and started the omelet to cooking again. The coffee was ready. He poured a cup and put in a sugar cube, stirred it and took a sip.

What now? It tasted very strange!

Shit! He'd put a boullion cube with garlic in it, not sugar!

There was a knock on the door. He grabbed the towel and wrapped it around him this time.

One of the religious nuts was there. He said they had possibly over-reacted when he came to the door nude. Perhaps he didn't dress in his own home, which was a bit strange, but not illegal. The way the guy stared it was obvious he hoped Phil would still be nude.

"You do believe in God, in Jesus Christ?" he intoned.

"In *a* God, yes. In Christ, no. I used to believe, but I know very well that God is a vicious sadistic monster. It's the only explanation for my life. This could not be happening without malicious direction."

"Er, um! You could ... I will leave some things with you. You will see that your life can become one of joy and salvation, not a sordid search for meaningless things and money and sex."

"I get by. I'm not after money or things. You, of course, would appreciate it if I could see a way to donate a few dollars to your cause to save the world from itself whether it wanted to be saved or not."

"Money and things, but sex? You would continue to seek physical pleasures, if not the material things?"

"Sure! Why not? No, I'm not interested in a little diversion right about now. It's too early in a miserable morning."

"Er, um! I, er, that is. Perhaps another time. I will leave a few things for you to read."

"Uh-huh. They go right to the circular file. I've read it all. It's bullshit. I really do have things to do. Excuse me if I don't care to hear your particular line that is the only true way. It's the same one forty other cults claim. Have a nice day." He closed the door in the idiot's face.

What was that smell?

He hadn't turned the stove off this time. The omelet was a coating of charcoal on the skillet.

He swore tiredly, cleaned the skillet and saw that he'd used the last two eggs.

No sweat! He had a bunch of chickens wandering around the yard all the time. Two had nests by the garage. He went out and got six eggs from the two nests and went back inside.

He put four of the eggs in the 'Fridge and held one over the pan to tap it with the back of a knife.

It exploded.

That one got to him! "Why me, Lord?" he asked of the ceiling – which had a bit of egg detritus here and there, as did the walls, cabinets, etc. He could smell that his hair was a little singed. He didn't think it was enough to show much.

Why didn't he react in a normal fashion to these things that happened that were so far from normal it was ridiculous? Was it his determination that God would have to come up with more and more things that were weirder and weirder to even get his attention?

He sighed and picked up the other egg. It didn't explode, at least. He held it away this time.

He went to the 'Fridge and got another egg. He inspected it. It was just an egg. He tapped it and had his omelet base. He put in the other things and put it on the stove and poured another cup of coffee. This time he made damned sure it was a sugar cube.

When the omelet was just right he rolled his eyes and turned it.

Okay! What was this shit? It turned like he was a professional!

"Oh, no! I'm am *not* going to believe anything has changed! You got me too many times before that way!" he declared.

The omelet was good. That was part of the scheme to get him to feeling his luck (or whatever) was changing. Not gonna work!

He finished the breakfast, dressed and went to work. He was a computer programmer. At least, his luck was normal in that. He couldn't support himself if that went the way everything else did.

Lunch time. He went to the café, Nancy's, where he sometimes ate. He would rather use the restaurant four blocks away, but it looked just enough like rain that he knew he'd get there just in time for the cloudburst of the century when he started back. He was onto a lot of it.

The food was okay, but the grease seemed a bit rancid they used to cook the French fries. He covered the taste with catsup – which he should have paid more attention to when he grabbed the bottle. It was half hot sauce and half catsup, by the taste.

No go, God! I like picante!

He finished, having sense enough to forego dessert in the place. It ranged from fair to horrible. He knew from long experience which one he'd get.

He got back to his office and was going into his cubicle when he had a sudden urgent need of the toilet. It was occupied, but Fledgers came out fairly quickly. He dashed in and sat. Lots of gas, lots of noise, lots of stink.

"Good one, God. You're getting sneakier."

He went back to his cubicle, warning the three others there that he may have to make emergency runs to the toilet. Beware!

"Ate at Nancy's on Monday? Thought you knew better!" Syd chided.

"I do. I forgot it's Monday. It was just like any day since I got up."

He finished the work day. Not much of note happened except the comp crashed when he had two hours of work on it to be lost. He was able to reformat it fast enough since he had all the basic right there to program in again.

He got home and fixed a light dinner, SSS – the gas and such hadn't been but the one time. He dressed and looked at himself in the mirror. Other than a burned patch in his hair on the right front he didn't look too bad.

He felt trepidation. This day had turned into one that was actually pleasant since the gas bout. He could expect the roof to fall in at any moment.

He got to Jennie's place barely on time – to find that there was no one there.

What now? She would have called if anything happened.

He hoped nothing had happened to her.

He took out his cell phone to call her. It was discharged. She had probably called him and gotten no response.

He went back home to put the phone on the charger and to call her. She answered and said she tried to call, but his phone was off. She called at his work. Some guy named Ralph said he'd pass the message on. She had to go to Memphis. Her mother had a heart attack and was critical.

Ralph had probably written a terse note and put it on his desk and forgotten it.

He considered going somewhere.

He'd have one drink and come back home. Birthdays weren't ever that much to him.

He went into the Palm Room at the Tropical Inn Hotel. He got a Cuba Libre and went out onto the terrace. There was an attractive woman at a table, alone. He went to start a conversation. Her boyfriend came up just after he'd said he was Phil. Would she like some company?

She did react to him like she was interested. More than interested. She answered that she was with someone, thank you. She managed to slip him a phone number. He read the slip when he went back inside. Jill Ames, 555-8886. Way to go!

He went back to finish his drink. He talked to the bartender, Jack. As he was finishing the drink Jill walked by and gave him a look when the boyfriend was paying the tab. He smiled.

When they went on, Jack came to say, "She's expensive and will steal anything loose. We don't like her working this place. She should be down around the pool halls in Pottertown."

It figured. He went home and to bed.

Why Me, Lord?

On the way home a taxi went through a puddle and splashed a lot of mud on him.

Happy fucking birthday!

<u>*Strange Visitor*</u>

In the morning, which was just a *little* better than the day before, Phil was whipping up pancakes when there was a knock on the door. He sighed. If it was that nut who hinted he'd like to get him in bed he was going to knock him on his ass! He thought it was plain enough he wasn't interested.

It wasn't him. It was some guy in a cheap suit. Probably begging. He was fit enough to work, so he wouldn't get a dime from Phil Fethers.

"I'm here on an investigation," he said quickly, noting the look on Phil's face. "Gordon Mills. Washington and Lincoln Investigative Srvices.

"What this is about is going to seem crazy to you. It does to me and I'm investigating it. It's about, believe it or not, chickens.

"I saw that this place has a lot of chickens wandering around and that it's not fenced with anything to keep them in or out. I need to know if any not yours have shown up the past few days.

"I know this sounds loopy. I don't know what it's about. I usually look for people or drugs or laundered money or whatever. Chickens is a first."

"I don't have any chickens, so don't pay much attention to them. There are a lot of things in the yard they like. It's the biggest lot this side of town and has two acres with nothing there. The chickens have nests around so I get all the fresh eggs I want. I don't mind having chicken gumbo or fried chicken once in awhile, either. They don't belong to anybody.

"Come on in. I'm fixing breakfast and will have to get to work right away. Maybe you can tell me what it's about. Chickens, I won't swallow! They're just ... oh."

"Oh?"

"Would these chickens lay eggs that explode?"

"You're putting me on because you think I'm putting you on. I swear I'm not."

"FBI asking me about chickens, doesn't make sense. FBI asking about chickens that lay exploding eggs almost does, considering what this country has become."

"I'm not FBI. I'm an independent investigator. It's not the FBI who hired me. It's another organization. I don't know why the FBI doesn't handle it."

Phil poured Gordon a cup of coffee and sat. He had to hear this one's story!

"Okay. Washington and Lincoln. How very original. It's not FBI, it's CIA. They aren't supposed to be inside the country. You're looking for chickens. I may know something. Whether or not I'll share the information depends on your answers.

"What do you know and what do you suspect. I can tell you're not sure whether or not you want anything to do with whatever it is."

"Fair enough. You're right about it being the CIA. I don't know anything about it except that a truckload of experimental chickens ran off the road and the cage door on one side came open. They got all but fourteen of the chickens. It was across Hiway Nine from here. You have chickens. They're flock animals. Likely starting place. You said something about eggs that explode. DUH!"

"Hmm. The CIA isn't allowed to do research in this country. They are. They've produced a chicken ... heh ...

that lays eggs that ex ... ex ...hee ... plode and they ....this is rich ...heh ... I wonder if the chickens will ex ... heh ... ha! ha! The Huh! Hee!" he broke down in laughter. Gordon stared at him.

"What the Hell?"

"I just pictured Mrs. Beaver in her apron and empty smile fixing a chi ... chi ... chicken for, heh! Dinner. She puts it in a pa ... pan and, hee, puts it in the hot ov ... ov ... oven and it, tuh, tuh, takes the side of the huh ... house ... out! Heeee! She's standing there with her huh ... huh hair singed ... and ... and black around ... around the eyes ... with a ...sur .... sur ... hee ... look .... hah, ha!"

This time Gordon broke down in hilarity too. They both laughed until they were crying.

"Some kids find a ... guh ... nest with eggs and ... thuh ... throw one at ... at ... a car ... and ... it ...guh ... takes the wi-wi ... winds ...shiel ... Ha,ha!"

"She looks like ... like that ... Budweiser ad where the ... hor ... horse farts ... across the ... candle ... that I saw ... before a ... a ...superbowl once. Just that ... that look! The hair fuzzed ... fuzzed out and ... heh ... singed ... and ... the expression ... ha, ha!"

"The driver ... sitting there ... with, guh ... that same ... expres .... expression! Ha! Like Wily Coyote when a buh buh bomb ex ... exp ...ha, ha!!"

They finally were able to control their laughter and sat back. They laughed so hard and so much Phil's lungs were aching. He wiped the tears off with the dish towel. They didn't say anything for a couple of minutes. They didn't dare!

"I wonder how they worded the request for the ... the ... heh ... grant!" Gordon asked. "Gentlemen – please give us ten million dollars so we can ... guh ... produce a chicken that ... that lays ... guh ... exploding ... hee! ... eggs! It'll save hav ... having to manu ... manufacture hand grenades!" They sat and giggled.

"I would like to know what was the object. It seems a bit odd, even for the CIA," Phil said. "I guess we'd better catch the ones laying the eggs, though. It was really a pretty forceful explosion. You can see the egg all over the room. I guess if the shell hit you edgewise it would cut."

"I have a thing that will tell me which ones. I think ... do you have a place to keep them?"

"Yeah. We can put wire across the woodshed. There's no wood in it."

"I want to see if I can find out what that bunch of clowns are doing before I give them their chickens back. I'd dearly love to hear the explanations. They'll probably be funnier than this."

They went out back where the chickens were picking around. Gordon took a meter with an antenna sticking out of it from his pocket and turned it on. It immediately started beeping.

Phil said he had to get to work. He showed Gordon the roll of chicken wire and the shed, then dressed and went.

When he came home there were twelve chickens in the shed. Four ordinary looking roosters and eight ordinary looking hens. Gordon had taken four orange crates and had made nests in them. Maybe he'd soon have his own collection of exploding eggs.

What in hell would he do with them?

He went in the house and fixed his dinner, then thought about the program he was working on, then watched some boring TV until he went to bed early.

The morning had been mixed. He'd slipped on a shoe and had a bruised elbow where it hit the dresser on the way down. The toilet was clogged again. There was some kind of obstruction in the drain.

He thought of flushing an egg. Maybe it would explode when it hit the obstruction. He could picture the water shooting out of the toilet and pictured someone sitting on a toilet when an egg exploded in the drain. He would be sitting on one of those Disney spouts with the weird surprised look. He giggled. Now he was going to think about exploding eggs when anything came up.

He had just finished breakfast when Gordon came in from the back carrying two eggs. "Want some fried eggs?" he asked. They both laughed.

"I didn't find much of anything," Gordon reported. "I have to do it with hints and suggestions. I was talking with the person who gave me the assignment. I said I had some hints that one person had a lot more chickens this week than she had three weeks ago. I asked if I should just poison them or something. He called a number and some Dr. Bossman came to ask about what I found. I just said it was a remark, but that was how I would find anything. Anybody who suddenly had a dozen more laying hens was going to try to see no one knew.

"He said I was not to harm the chickens. They needed them to finish the research, so I suggested I would find them and just break any eggs they'd laid to be sure whoever had them didn't raise the chicks and breed their own whatever.

"I was told, very nervously, that I was to handle any eggs with extreme care. That's what they really need from those hens. He gave me a number to call immediately if I found any. He would come to gather the eggs, himself. In person. To see there was no lost research, don't you know, Old Sock! It didn't seem to occur to him that anyone who had the eggs would sell them or cook them. People don't just leave them there in the nests."

"They live in some kind of fantasy world. Maybe we can arrange to find one of the hens and where she had laid a couple eggs. You could call him. I would very naturally want to know why some scientist guy wanted my chickens and eggs. It might be fun to hear the story."

"Or it might occur to them you know too much already so they should eliminate that kind of problem before it cropped up. Be careful. I know those people and the way they, excuse the expression, think."

"I can thwart them in that. I'm not the kind of person they're used to dealing with."

They made a plan. Gordon and Phil were going to be buddies and a team. Phil didn't fall for that one, either ... still, Gordon had the hens and eggs so he would tend to handle the problem if he was that type.

"Why, wouldn't it be a streak of fantastic luck for them to have found a computer genius who could save them years in their resarch?" he asked, innocently.

Gordon grinned and giggled. "What would be your guarantee that you wouldn't accidentally give them some kind of idea that might work?"

"Not in the equation. If you knew me, you'd see that!

"Let's work out how we do it."

Stroke of Luck

Phil had always had a very large supply of luck. He was known to admit it and to say it was a pity it was all bad. He was going to go way out on a limb and trust that it would continue as it always had been.

He called Jennie to ask how she was doing. She said she was going to be stuck in Memphis for at least a month. She would appreciate it if he would take care of her place. Feed the goldfish and that kind of thing. The yard wasn't big, so it wouldn't be hard to maintain. He could stay there if he liked. She trusted him. He was her closest friend in all the world.

He agreed. She said the key to the back door was under the pot of begonias by the steps. The other keys, the spare set, were in the cutlery drawer in the kitchen, first on the left of the stove.

Damn it! This wasn't his bad luck streak!

He knew what to do! He called Gordon and said to meet him tonight. They were going to move a chicken and a couple of eggs to a new home. He had time coming. They would arrange for Gordon to call Dr. Bossman tomorrow to come try to convince him he should be allowed to take the chickens. Gordon said he found out about these, but couldn't just steal them or anything because too many people would ask too many questions. It was his job to find the chickens. He said to call him when he did. It was now up to him.

Phil moved one hen and one rooster to Jennie's back yard. He and Gorden spent a little time making a cage with a wooden box for a roost. The smaller box with the nest was inside. He bought a big sack of chicken feed. Phil managed to hit his thumb with a hammer and to cut his other hand with a saw and to tear his pants on a nail and spill water down the front of his pants that looked like he'd pissed in them. Everything was perfectly normal.

They decided to call Bossman at seven thirty. Gordon would say, "... was waiting when he got home from work. He says he has a chicken. Two. He caught them beside a public road and isn't about to give them to anybody. He can have a fresh egg every morning from his own back yard! He doesn't need money. He's damned suspicious why anybody would offer a hundred bucks apiece for chickens he caught by the side of the road. There were a dozen there, at least. He told me to fuck off."

"Dr. Bossman, I agreed to find the chickens. The rest is up to you. I'm going out where he caught them to see if I can find them."

"No way! Half the town knows about them. He'll probably tell them about me offering a hundred bucks apiece. Half the town will be out there tomorrow to try to catch a hundred dollar chicken!"

"If I did that you'd really have some questions you dare not answer. I'm not about to put my neck on that block!"

"I'll tell him you'll be here. I don't think he works tomorrow, or that he'll work here. He's a research computer expert or something. The way he talked he knows exactly who I am. I talked to him at five at his office, he's said some things that no one knows."

"He's a *computer* expert. He can find anything it would take us a month to find in ten minutes."

"I'll run over and tell him."

"I can think of a lot of ways that would solve more than

the one problem. Who knows. He might even be able to save you ten years of research because you asked the right question the right way or something."

"I'll be out there at dawn. I may be able to find the rest of them."

He hung up and grinned. "He'll be here about nine in the morning. I think he'll want to hire you, which means he would get the chickens and maybe the one who could help him make the breakthrough of the century in genetic splicing. We know how they're doing it. We have to learn why."

"I worry. Things are going right. They never do."

"What the Hell? Like you finding chickens by the road. Maybe you could find facts by the computer. Tell him you're at the point in your work where you could make thousands a week from the contracts. He'll offer thousands a week to work for him, plus you would be free to pursue your own path part time, is the way he put it."

"Where will he get thousands a week to pay me?"

"Same place he gets his. The taxpaying schmucks."

Phil gave him the old one finger salute.

"Yes? That Gordon character said you would come today to explain why you want my damned chickens."

Dr. Bossman was a short, plump man with salt and pepper hair who wore steel frame glasses. His clothes didn't quite fit him. He had a soldier bring him in a military Jeep.

"Yes, yes," he replied testily. "They're research subjects that escaped from a truck. I hope you have not eaten any of the eggs from those chickens. It could be, er, dangerous. Chemical contamination, you see. It's why we have to get them all back.

"You said there were more than a dozen? You told Gordon exactly where they were?"

"Yeah. It was a couple of weeks ago. They're probably all over the county now, the ones that haven't ended up as somebody's chicken soup."

"Oh, I hope not!" he cried. "Well, eating the chickens themselves probably wouldn't hurt anyone. It's the eggs that are of concern."

"Why?"

"If you break them open they could, uh, release a very toxic gas. Or something. Nobody must open one of those eggs!"

"Well, I didn't check the nest the last couple of days.. Chickens will stop laying if they have a fright or something. We can see if this one's laid any."

He led Bossman out to the little cage. They went in and to the nest. Where there were two eggs they put in yesterday, there were now three.

"They are laying eggs! Oh, dear! Oh, dear!"

Phil reached into the nest and got the three eggs. They headed back to the house. Phil put the eggs in a plastic container and set them on the porch rail. Bossman said he would take the eggs to the Jeep and would return to tell Phil how important their research was. Phil handed the container to Bossman. He managed to slip just then and one egg rolled out of the container (with his help) and across the concrete post by the steps. He grabbed for it. Bossman held the container like it would try to escape by itself.

The egg rolled off the post and fell the two or three feet below the porch level to land in a clump of fern. The fern was in the rocks. The path went down from there for another two steps before the level ground. The egg rolled out and dropped on a rock by the path.

There was an explosion a little more forceful than when he tapped the egg. Bossman squealed like a stuck pig. Phil faked a surprised-shocked look.

Phil turned to Bossman. "I think the explanation for that isn't going to be easy to swallow. Shall we go inside and have a little talk?"

Bossman called the soldier and gave him the two remaining eggs. The soldier asked about the explosion he just heard. Bossman said he demonstrated a thing for use in running crows away from crops. Those eggs were part of the research. Handle them with extreme care. Phil and he went inside, where Phil poured them each a cup of coffee.

"Well?"

"I am a geneticist. We spliced genes into the chickens that produce two very reactive chemicals. They are sensitive to shock and will react from a shock that would break the shell. The research from that point is to make the shells contain a compound much like an acrylic. It would...."

"... making the explosion throw six very sharp, hard blades at high velocity. The blades could kill the person cracking the egg," Phil explained to Gordon.

"Cripes! What would they do with anything like that?"

"Use them for assassinations of terrorist leaders, anywhere. He gets up, does the SSS bit, then goes into the kitchen to have his breakfast. A good percent of the time that includes eggs. Boom. One less problem for our government, no connection. Oh, boo-hoo."

"Would it work?"

"Yes, except for the little detail that kind of idiot always misses."

"Such as?"

"How many powerful world leaders go in the kitchen in the morning to cook their own breakfast? Maybe they could kill off the leaders' chefs."

They were going to get the giggles again. Gordon changed the subject. "So? What's the offer to you?"

"Well, he has his limits. I projected I would make five thousand a week from what I'm working on. He said that was within the budget. I could continue with what I was working on in my spare time, which would be most of it. They will give me room, board and all that, plus the five grand is tax exempt.

"I said I'd consider it."

"Will you?"

"Sure! Two months at that and I'll have enough to do several things I want to do."

"Once in you can never get out. That's why I'm an independent contractor."

"Which is just what I'd be."

"You'll still know too much. Be careful."

Phil nodded seriously.

Now to see where this fiasco would lead. The one thing certain about it was that it would supply enough laughs for enough years to be worth it. Phil did always retain his sense of humor and the ridiculous. He laughed a lot.

After Bossman left he had gone back to his place. He had seven eggs in the nest boxes there.

He wondered if they had a long shelf life. That gave him the giggles again. He wandered around, fixed a few things around the house he had been putting off, then went back to Jennie's to feed the chickens. He pulled a few weeds in her spice garden.

He was stuck wondering what to do with his time. He could maybe set up a website for the independent farmers.

Chicken farmers? It would have a forum and blogs. That could get Bossman's bowels in an uproar! He could put a test run question something like: *I would like some advice from those who raise chickens commercially.*

I raise corn for the cattle feed industry and admit I don't know much about chickens. Several chickens wandered into my barn, I guess because of all that corn, and stayed. It was okay. I like eggs as much as the next guy and chicken soup is a good change now and then.

What I want to know is if their shit or something can explode. They stay in the loft at night and have nests in the hay up there. Two times something has blown up. It's costing me a lot to have to fix all that stuff. How do you keep that from happening? Is it something in their diet? I heard about feeding them gunpowder, but always thought that was just a tale.

Would that cause a panic or what?

He got the giggles. He pictured some farmer going out to the barn in the morning and finding a big hole where a whole nest full of eggs exploded and took the roof off. The tractor looked like a bazooka hit it!

Would Bossman read something like that and believe it? What would he do?

Let's see. The eggs explode with a force of a quarter stick of fifty percent dynamite. If there were three eggs and one fell out of the loft it would explode. That wouldn't be enough ... oh, dear me! The concussion would cause the other eggs in the building to detonate! Oh, dear me! I never figured on something like this! They weren't supposed to have their nests in a loft! Let me see. If we raise a thousand hens and they all lay an egg and we store them in a warehouse what happens if someone drops one right there in the building? Oh, dear me! It would be like when the arsenal in Iraq went up! It would take out a city block, at least!

Oh, well. We'll just be sure we raise them where there aren't any close neighbors. Problem solved!

Phil shook his head. That would be about the reaction he could expect. About two days later he would stop all of a sudden. "Oh, dear me! That means we didn't find all of those chickens when the truck turned over! They're breeding! This could be worse than killer bees!"

The CIA would have to come up with a cover story. There would have to be a goat.

News Date

Pres. Bossman of the Washington and Lincoln Research center in Podunk, Mississippi, has been arrested and charged with being a mad scientist. The recent scare because of a few silly pitiful minor little incidents with exploding eggs has been traced to Dr. Bossman, who had some wild and crazy scheme from his fevered insanity to take over the army by producing chickens that lay eggs that will explode. No one can understand the reasoning behind the insane idea.

"While Dr. Bossman has done some independent contract work with government agencies, he does not and did not represent any agency that operates within the borders of the United States of America and I didn't know anything about it, so you sure as heck can't blame me for

anything I didn't ever even dream was happening!" President Smith answered forcefully when asked if he was aware of the incidents. "I had not heard anything about this before your questions right here. I have asked congress to investigate the matter. I imagine what work he did was for the administration before mine. You are aware of the depths to which that party will sink. They will undoubtably attempt to charge this administration with something or other, but I tell you right now it will be false and that such specious charges will come to nothing."*

We will report immediately on any further developments in the case.

In other words, you could expect typical political double-talk. It won't occur to any of the reporters to ask how he has congress investigating something he didn't know about until their questions right there.

He went back to his place. He was a bit nervous about his long spate of normal to good luck. The higher he got, the longer and harder the fall.

He locked Jennie's place carefully, then went out the front gate. He heard someone call his name and looked up as he was closing it and managed to slam it on his hand. He looked around, but didn't see anyone who had called to him.

A truck was dumping a load of topsoil on a lawn down the block. He probably heard someone calling about where to dump the fill or something.

He turned toward his place and stepped on something that almost dumped him on his ass. Dog shit! He swore rather colorfully and looked up from the crap to see the four from the church standing there with shocked looks on their faces.

Nothing to lose now. "People who let their damned dogs shit on the fucking sidewalk should be horsewhipped," he said pleasantly. He walked on. He heard the one who had come back to his house say, "It's a test from God. It has to be!"

A kid on a bicycle flew around the corner where a hedge cut off the view and knocked him down. He couldn't very well knock a seven or eight year old girl on her ass. He said she shouldn't be riding her bike on the sidewalk.

She said, "Fuck you! " Got on her bike and rode away.

Hell! A big black streak down his pants!

It started raining. It wasn't an ordinary rain, it was the storm of the year. It had to be!

He dashed across the street and slipped on the wet sidewalk on the corner, falling into two trash cans there. One had some rotten meat or something such in it that smelled like ... rotten meat.

He got up and said, "Welcome back, God! I missed you!"

Why did he get a feeling of comradery? He was as nuts as a loon!

He managed to survive the rest of the way home. He'd left two windows open. The bedroom was soaked.

Yep! Things were back to normal! He wouldn't turn a hair if lightning struck all those exploding eggs out back and made a mess of the neighborhood.

He pictured a snow of feathers. The chickens were right there. It would solve the chicken round-up.

He plugged in the coffee pot. It made a "pfffftt" sound and burned out.

He sighed and put the coffee in a pan of water and put it on the stove.

No gas. As much as expected. It didn't bother him. He took out a hotplate and put the pan on it. He had two more he got on sale when Harpner's went out of business.

"God, you just have to come up with something new. This is getting boring."

He cooked a steak from the Fridge on the hotplate and ate it with a bag of potato chips and some lettuce salad. He then puttered around the computer for awhile, then showered and went to bed. It had been quite a day!

There must have been a bitch in heat close. A pack of dogs spent three hours barking and fighting all over the property until he went out with his slingshot and popped a couple of them. They went down the property to where they could keep him awake without being in range of his slingshot. He contemplated getting the .22 out and picking about ten of them off.

He'd end up in jail for discharging a firearm in an occupied area. He knew better.

He went back to bed. Those damned dogs would bark all night. He was thinking of poisoning every dog in the neighborhood, which he would never do, as tempting as it seemed at the moment. He smirked to himself and put on a bathrobe, then went out to the woodshed. There were four eggs in the nests.

He threw one toward the dogs. He had a good arm. It hit right in the middle of the pack.

Oh, shit! He ran into the house and turned on a light in the bedroom, then went out front to look down the road toward the corpses of four or five dogs scattered along the road. The neighbor from that end across the road was just coming to his gate.

The best defense ... "What did you do, Tom?" he asked.

"Whatever that was, you should get the citizenship medal. Those damned dogs were driving me crazy! If the cops come or anything I'll say a car went by, there was a 'boom' and it kept right on going."

"I didn't do anything! I was thinking of ... maybe it happened just like that. Whatever, it got rid of some of them! I wish it could have been twenty more of them!"

"Yeah. Whoever, I'll pay for another grenade if they'll use it! I wish I had the guts!"

They chatted a few minutes. No cops came. They decided the county truck would pick the dogs up in the morning.

This time Phil managed to get to sleep. He would tell Gordon he found a good use for the eggs in the morning.

<u>*Another Ho-hum Day*</u>

Phil was fixing his eggs (not those) for breakfast when Bossman and Gordon came rushing in. Bossman said there was the sound of an explosion last night. It was on this property – and why wasn't he at the house where they'd talked?

"A bitch in heat had dogs barking all night. Tom or somebody threw a grenade at them." Gordon was behind Bossman and grinned at Phil, who wasn't having complete success at hiding his laughter. Bossman didn't seem to notice.

"The truck with the chickens turned over just a few hundred feet from here on Hiway nine," Bossman said. "We feared something ... but it's a relief to know it wasn't that."

"It could have been," Phil pointed out. "The dogs running around. A nest in the grass. Boom!"

"Gheeee!"

"I wasn't at the other place last night because my girlfriend who lives there is in Memphis. I live here. I take care of her place when she's away."

"But why did you take the chickens there? There are a lot of them outside here right now!"

"Because these aren't mine. I can keep mine in a cage there and the eggs are mine. Not that I want those particular eggs."

"Oh. I see. Well, I suppose Gordon checked all of these so they aren't ... but then, where did the egg that the dogs broke come from?"

"That was only a possibility. The chickens come and go.

Maybe one came and went."

"I'll check the ones outside," Gordon said. He went out. Phil offered coffee to Bossman, who sat at the table and looked harried. He said he wished he'd never heard of those damned particular genes.

"Dr. Bossman, how would you store the eggs? Would they retain their potency?"

"Oh, refrigerate them and they aren't sensitive. The chemicals will break down naturally in about three weeks without refrigeration. We worked out everything that can happen."

"Except for a truck that runs off the road."

"Yes. That was unforeseen. I hope it is the only thing. I have some hesitation before inserting the acrylic-producing gene."

They chatted a bit. Gordon came in with a hen and a rooster. He said they had wandered in sometime. Maybe that's where the dog egg came from. There were fourteen lost. They had two here and two at the other place, which meant they only had to find ten more. That was to tell Phil this accounted for all of them. There were ten in the woodshed.

"I guess we'd better get on back. I'll come here this afternoon to see if any more wander in. I'll spend this morning checking out things I've heard," Gordon suggested, rolling his eyes toward Bossman.

Yeah. It would be a good idea to get him out of there before he thought of looking over the place.

Phil walked them to the door. He saw the other three eggs from last night on the table there. Gordon spotted them and pointed to water in the hall, drawing Bossman's attention. He said there was water there. Phil said it was an open window with yesterday's rain. He was going to mop it up this morning.

They got Bossman out without him spotting the eggs.

They drove off. Phil went with them to the Jeep. There was still some mud around so he got some on him when the wheels spun in a puddle.

"Good to know I can always depend on you, God! Good morning!" He went back inside. He took the mattress from the big bed outside into the sunlight. It was soaked. It would take a couple of days to dry out. Lucky he had the guest room to stay in until things were back to as close to normal as they would get.

He remembered those eggs. He put them in the Fridge. Bossman said they were safe if they were cold.

He slammed the door to the Fridge. The eggs weren't cold yet. There was a loud "Mmmppfth!" sound and the door flew open. The sides of the Fridge were puffed out slightly. The insulation absorbed most of the shock.

"Shit!" he said, dejectedly.

He cleaned up the mess. The door fit alright. It sealed. The Frdige looked a bit weird, sort of rounded. It seemed to keep right on working. Only one of the eggs exploded, it seemed. Not all of those hens were laying the spliced eggs. It did blow all the stuff in the Fridge into a gooey mess of a ball.

"You're going to have to think up things that don't make such a mess. I could get irritated."

He finally had the place in good shape and clean. Gordon came and said he had no choice about those two chickens. The driver saw him catch them. No loss.

"Yeah. I did find a good use for them. I can tell you the eggs aren't so easy to set off if they're cold, but I guess you knew that. Don't put them in the refrigerator and slam the door. Wait until they're cold for that. I can also tell you not all of them will explode."

Gordon looked at the Fridge. He shook his head, then couldn't hide a giggle. Phil giggled in turn, then they laughed and made up scenarios where the eggs exploded. Gordon decided he'd "find" one or two chickens a day.

Tom called the county about the dead dogs. They picked them up. The man on the truck asked if he could expect more. Tom told him he hoped so, but they don't know who did it. They would buy him another grenade or two.

"They won't be back tonight. They form packs when there's a bitch in heat. That would be the black and white one. She got the hardest hit."

"That works as well, " Phil said. "Just so we can get some sleep. They ought to make people keep their dogs home."

"That's the law, but nobody pays it any mind. It works alright. They won't make too much of a stink if you reduce the canine population. Claim their dog, pay a fifty buck fine."

Phil went to Jennie's to feed his chickens and be sure everything was alright in the house. He got a new tank of gas for the stove at home and bought a few things he needed. He decided he was going to make five grand a week, so he bought a good mattress. The delivery truck was there so he rode home with the mattress. It was a good one, and expensive. OrthoPerfect model A100. Eight hundred thirty nine bucks!

He thoroughly expected that he wasn't going to get the job, now that he spent the money. What the Hell? He had enough saved up that it wouldn't hurt.

He worked around the yard for a couple of hours, then went in to fix lunch. He flipped on the TV to see "... this OrthoPerfect model A100 for only three hundred fifty dollars, today only! Less than half the original price! Limited number in stock!"

Okay! The job would probably be there. He lost about what could be expected if things were truly back to what was normal for him. He was learning how to use what was happening to him.

Don't get smug.

He hooked up the gas, or started to. This tank was from another distributor and didn't fit his regulator.

He took the other regulator and hose from the drawer, hooked it up and had the stove again. Another place where he was prepared for things that were bound to happen to him.

"You're slipping! Old lady driving you up the walls, God?"

Maybe he had one like those old Greek gods. A harridan of a wife. He giggled at the thought. He could picture Michaelangelo's God saying, "It ain't funny!" with a miserable look on his face.

He reached into the cabinet for the flour. He moved his hand around until he hit the mouse trap. Pain time! It was a good thing it wasn't a rat trap! That would have broken fingers instead of just hurting.

A lot of these thing were from his own mind. He knew the trap was there. He knew to close the windows before he left.

A lot weren't. He had to pay more attention to his own short-comings to get much relief. He had to be wary about those things he didn't do to himself.

He went to the woodshed to collect the seven eggs there. He was careful when he put them in the Fridge. No slamming doors.

He had the whole afternoon. He would go fishing.

He got to the lake on the bus. He walked to where he liked to fish where he sat on the log there to rig his reel. The log had rotted enough on the end that it dropped off the rock and dumped him in the mud. He swore. This was going to be a normal – for him – trip.

He saw some swirls a little to the left and went through the willows to be able to cast into the action on the water. The first cast tangled in the branches above him. He got it worked loose and made a perfect cast into the action. Strke!

He pulled in a carp. No good! He turned it loose.

He cast a few more times. He got another strike, but the line broke and he lost his favorite lure.

He headed back to his spot. He slipped on a rock by the water and ended up in the lake. He climbed out to get tangled in the willow branches. He worked his way to the log. His cap was missing.

He saw it floating out into the lake. Shit!

He cast a few times, then changed lures again.

First cast he caught a nice bass he put on a stringer. He cast a few more times and got a strong hit. He fought the fish in.

A catfish? They almost never hit top water lures!

Oh, well. He threw it back and sat on the log (he had put another rock under the hard part) to have a cold beer, only it wasn't cold. The ice had melted and run out. He ate some soggy cheese crackers with it.

He moved around a bit, but didn't see any likely spots, so

went back to the log. His stringer was gone.

There were several kids playing around the area. He should have known better than to leave if far.

He fished some more and caught another bass. He made a stringer with a piece of polypropylene he carried. He moved around a bit more, not going where he couldn't see the stringer. He made a few more casts, but nothing was biting. He got a backlash that made knots of the nylon. He swore and worked on it for a minute, then swore again. He decided to go back home.

The first bus got one look at him as it stopped. The door closed in his face and it drove off. He gave it the one finger salute.

A half hour later the bus stopped. He was prepared with a black garbage bag, so put it on the seat to sit on. The driver thanked him for being considerate of other people. About two percent of his riders were. When he got home a little after five he was drenched and muddy and his favorite fishing shirt was beyond salvation. He'd lost his lucky fishing cap. He reel was jammed up with nylon in hundreds of knots. His favorite lure was gone.

And with a nice bass for supper. There was always that one tiny redeeming factor. He would cut the nylon from the reel and put on new. He had several old shirts for fishing, as well as pants. His only loss that he cared about was his fishing cap, but he caught his supper after it was lost. He caught supper on another lure.

All in all, another ho-hum day.

He piddled around, got another egg from the woodshed, worked on the farm website, watched fifteen minutes of stupidly extreme karate and bombs and bullets and went to bed. The mattress smelled new, but was as comfortable as advertised.

Why hadn't Gordon come back?

He reached for the phone to call. There was no answer.

He laid back down. Three minutes later the phone rang.

It was Jennie. She just got the strangest call. Flo Jenkins, next door to her place there, said there was some kind of explosion at her place and something about dead chickens. What was that about?

"I don't know. Maybe ... an explosion? Chickens?

"I put two chickens in a little cage I made there until Gordon, a friend, could pick them up to take to, uh, his place out of town. I was fishing at the lake until five or so. I hadn't heard anything about any explosion. I was there this morning to check things out and to feed the chickens.

"That big white lily thing by the steps is blooming. I guess you'll miss it. It only blooms for a week or so. I'll take a picture and e-mail it to you." Change the subject and see what the Hell was going on!

She chattered about how she knew he would take better care of her place than she did. Blah, blah, boring blah. After ten minutes or ten hours or eternity he was able to get her off the phone.

Should he go to her place?

Tomorrow.

He went back to bed.

Tomorrow's Petty Pace

He got up to no aches and pains in the morning. That was a new one! Maybe getting rid of that old mattress was his good decision for this month!

He managed to not hurt himself seriously through breakfast, then called Gordon again. No answer.

Go to Jennie's. Find out if there's a connection.

His phone rang. It was Gordon. He said the police had his phone. He could only use it when one of them was there. He didn't have much time. Things would work out okay. His boss would get him out. He'd explain later. Charging him with animal cruelty was just plain ridiculous! He didn't know there were any chickens there! He just set off a crow bomb at dusk because the damned things were roosting in that big pecan tree! How the hell would he know Jennifer had chickens! She was in Memphis! Got to go!

That explained a lot.

He got the giggles. What had probably happened was that hen laid an egg. The nest crate was about two feet off the ground. Something had dropped the egg out of the nest. Boom!

He pictured the hen, Disney style, clucking and laying an egg, the egg falling, and the surprised look and feathers falling all around. He giggled. He could picture God again saying, "It ain't funny!" He got the giggles.

Not too much happened on the way to Jennie's. He saw the mess that had been the cage. Flo came over to ask what had happened. He said he wasn't sure. He thought a can of starting fluid blew up. It was mostly ether, you know. If the press valve leaked a little it took almost nothing to ignite ether.

She went back to her place. Phil's phone rang. Gordon was out. Bossman had pulled some strings somehow. They had to explain that explosion better than a crow bomb. Those were all noise.

"I told Flo, next door, it was probably starting fluid that leaked. Ether. Boom! Get a can and take it out somewhere and make it blow, then come here and 'find' it."

"Good thinking! Done! How did you explain it being there?"

"Didn't. Maybe for the lawn mower. It's hard to start.

"How do you suppose it happened? Why were you here? Did you see or hear anything?"

"I wasn't far. Bossman had a transmitter hidden there. A bug. He heard it and called me. I went over just in time for the cops to come and catch me trying to get rid of the feathers and such. I figured there might be an egg. There are too many chicken snakes around there. They eat the eggs. Probably, one got in the nest and dropped the egg out. I'll check for a dead snake."

Phil said he'd wait. He went around the place. He found a dead chicken snake about two feet long tangled in twisted chicken wire. It was easy to figure. It wasn't big enough to swallow the egg. It had tried and had knocked the egg out of the nest.

Gordon came about an hour later. He had a twisted starting fluid can that was ripped open along the seam. He tossed it among the mess and said the police would come over with Bossman in a little while. Bossman would "find" the can and explain about the lawn mower. Phil would say he bought a can and had used it once. It was back there somewhere. Maybe something turned it over and the press valve was hit, making a slow leak. Something caused a spark or whatever.

So it didn't make sense. It would go down as the cause of the explosion, let's go have a beer.

"Why is your head bleeding?" Gordon asked.

"It is?" he put his hand up to his head. Gordon said the other side. There was blood.

"I suppose it was from the chicken wire when I found the snake."

"Put some antibiotic on it."

They waited. Bossman came with a fat policeman. They went through the cage. Bossman "found" the ether can. The cop found the snake. Gordon said the can was probably on the shelf (that they couldn't say wasn't there amid the wreckage), the snake went along the shelf and knocked the can off. The can landed upside down, which broke the press valve off. It was ether. Something set it off. The cop was more than ready to make that suggestion in his report. Shake hands, say what a great job they'd done on this investigation and go.

Gordon and Bossman were undecided as to what to do next. Bossman said they had to find the rest of those chickens. Phil said that was their problem. He would do what he could.

"Oh. Yes. Well, now that you work for us you can aid Gordon in the search. I put you on the book as starting today."

They agreed. Bossman called his driver and left. Gordon and Phil cleaned up the mess and had the yard back to much as it had been before this fiasco. They decided they would find the rest of the chickens today. There was no way this particular type of research could ever become practical. It would give Phil a very good start at his new job.

Why Me, Lord?

What Next, Lord?

Phil Fethers stretched and looked in the mirror. It was a little crooked, so he reached to straighten it. It fell off the hook and crashed to the floor. It was stainless steel, so didn't break.

"Good morning! I was onto that one years ago. Old lady giving you Hell again?"

He nicked himself shaving. He put antibiotic cream on it. No chances.

The coffee pot got knocked off the stove, but he had a full cup. He gave it the bird and turned it upright. There was still more than a cup in it. He mopped the coffee up and put the eggs on the stove. The omelet looked perfect until he turned it. It then looked like scrambled eggs with vegetables. The toaster stuck and he had two sheets of charcoal when he popped it up. He dropped them in the garbage and put in two more slices. There was a humming noise, then the lights went out.

He unplugged the toaster and went to flip on the breaker.

Today made three months at the job. He was told the job would probably end in less than six months, but that would give him time to finish his project.

He guessed so. He would start it at any minute!

Bossman was being transferred to the Arizona facility. It was too dangerous to be handled anywhere other than the desert with no one within fifty miles.

He smirked to himself. Today the computer would make it necessary for Bossman to start another project. He had checked interdepartmental to find more than twenty million dollars had been wasted on Operation Igeldy

Pigeldy Project.

He sat to write the "Findings" of his special program to detect odds of a project working to specs.

The experimental insertion of genetic material into chickens is successful and has added much to scientific bases. The project is a success in producing more than was spent, though that production is in the scientific end, not the military.

The apparent success in inserts to produce an acrylic-like substance is as valuable, but for other uses.

The factors behind the original purpose of the experiments were lacking in finalization. The process was decreed practical for the production end, but the practical use end was faulty. The fact the product was there for use was negated by the fact that it was a use that was not practical. Suggest termination of project.

Factor not investigated properly: Terrorist leaders do not prepare their own food.

Phil sat back and read it over, then put it on a memory stick for his computer to find and report.

He went out front to find a group of church people coming down the road. He would be the second stop.

He got an evil grin on his face and went back inside.

There was soon a knock on his door. He went to throw the door open. Two of the women gasped and backed down the sidewalk toward the road. One gave him an appraising look, then slowly did the same. The one man with them looked like he would faint. He turned and walked away without a word.

Phil grinned and closed the door. This was another bunch who wouldn't be back.

"I can play a few little tricks like this against your

competition, huh?"

He got the comrady feeling for the second time.

Weird.

He would look for another project. He had enough to live on for awhile. Maybe he could make a big coop on the property and raise chickens for eggs.

Nah! He giggled at the idea.

He still needed a new project. He could probably get in with the government. He could get in touch with Gordon, who would know a few of the silly things they were up to.

He realized he was standing nude in the doorway when a car went by and swerved nearly off the road.

He went inside. He could smell ... something?

Oh. The lye. He had put half the can into the toilet. He was deter-mined he would get it unclogged to the point it would stay unclogged. That burnt smell may mean it had burned out whatever was in the way.

He went in to see the water in the bowl bubbling almost like it was boiling. The lye was damned sure eating something away!

There was a gurgle, then the water went down the drain, leaving a dirty brown glop in the bottom.

He flushed it. The new water would ... blow out and all over the bathroom! It was mostly steam and vapors that left a brownish coating on everything.

Good one, Lord! I have to admit I didn't expect that one!

Did he hear a giggle?

What? You forgot I tiled this whole bathroom for just such an eventuality?

He went to the closet, took out the garden hose, hooked it to the spigot outside the back door and washed the bathroom down. It was about time to clean it, anyway.

He coiled the hose and put it back, then looked into the toilet. It should have stopped boiling by now, but it was even hotter.

Lye is a base. He got the large bottle of vinegar from the kitchen and poured some of it into the boiling water.

Oh, shit! You can't add an acid to a hot base! It'll ... it did. It got so hot it cracked the toilet.

There was another gurgle. The water went down the drain.

He would buy another toilet. He knew how to do that kind of plumbing.

He rinsed the bathroom down again, got his tools, and took the old toilet out. He used the time to clean the area. While it was open like that he would run a snake down the line. He would be damned sure there wasn't anything obstructing it now!

See, Lord? I can turn almost any of it to a good result.

He opened the vent and left the door open with the big fan blowing in to dry it, then headed for the dealer for a new toilet. The lavatory was dirty and old. He had the money. He bought everything new.

<u>*A New Assignment*</u>

Phil looked at the gleaming new bathroom. He decided it was really all for the best.

Back to what he was doing when this started. He needed a new project.

He called Gordon, who said he had gotten some questions about what they had done and what he knew. He told them Phil was as good a security risk as they would ever find. He knew when to keep his mouth shut.

"Their computers told them you were the best man to look into feasibility studies. Didn't your own program tell them that, had they gotten in touch with you beforehand, those millions spent on something with no military application would have been saved?

"If it ain't got military application they ain't interested."

"Well, I hope they ... could someone accidentally suggest having me design programs to look for things that were missed in the programs they're running now?"

"What?"

"Maybe a program that would actually give them what they're after could be found to be faulty?"

He grinned. "I've heard rumors about some crazy nuclear thing out of a horror show they're sniffing around. A couple of really top scientists are very worried about it because it could work.

"From what I heard, it could kill all animal life and not damage buildings or plants or whatever. The one I overheard was saying it had a range of almost a mile. The problem would be finding a way to keep it in a sharp focus. They were saying something about director magnets or something."

Phil shrugged. They went to his computers. He checked the secret coded databases he'd learned about with the egg job, as he called it. There really was something like that proposed.

He checked finances/military/research. If it was Project Flashlight, there was already four million spent on primary research.

He introduced a secondary file. It was something they would find. Something that had been there all along, but was ignored. He put in a key that would come up within a day.

The net went down. He was sure it had been sent.

Lord, if you're doing that, this is too serious for games, okay?

The net came back online. That really did shock him.

Nah!

He worked a bit, then went in to fix dinner. Gordon had left an hour ago.

There was some stuff in the Fridge. He opened the door. The smell of rotted meat almost knocked him down.

He hadn't been home yesterday. He didn't get anything from it last night or this morning.

He sighed. He needed a new one, anyhow. It could have waited until after lunch.

He had some bread. Moldy.

A can of tuna and some egg noodles later he headed for the appliance store. He bought a new Fridge with a larger freezer.

When he got home there was a man standing by the door. A man in a cheap dark blue suit with black patent leather shoes.

"Mr. Fethers?"

"Yeah. Come on in. Tell me what it's about. Try to string me and you get nowhere."

He looked at Phil, then shrugged. "I'm Nort Green. What gave me away?"

"You're wearing a goddamned uniform! What the hell do you mean?"

"But ... oh. You worked with us. You know ... it isn't important. I wasn't going to try to snow you. I just have to ask you to do a little job for the department. They want to know something about the feasibility of research. We feel you could possibly save us a lot of time and funding if the projects won't produce more than they cost."

"You should have had that program going for years. You would have a lot of stuff you don't have and would probably have a few billion to play around with.

"The Flashlight Project kind of thing?"

"I don't know what. I ... never heard of that one. That could mean it's what it's about. You do know how we operate. I'll check. It should shake somebody up if you know about it."

He took out a large cell phone and made a call. He went down the sidewalk a distance. He gave Phil a strange look, then came to hand him the phone.

"Mr. Fethers, just where did you hear about the *non-existent* Flashlight Project?"

"On the net. There was some stuff on a forum or something."

There was a long silence. Phil shrugged and was handing the phone back to Nort when the voice continued.

"The net? It was on the net?"

"Yeah. Somewhere. I just mentioned that one. There was

talk about Project Silk Purse and HAARP and all that."

"Silk Purse? I don't ... but those are top secret! So is Flashlight!"

"That kind of thing is on the web as soon as someone thinks of it. (Phil had an idea. This would be fun!) England with their 'Derby Hat' Project and their New Flower Project and such. France with the Fleu de Lis and Germany with Ach Tung! and Russia with Yastrovia are out months before the departments they go to have a hint. Governments can't hide that kind of thing when they don't understand how the net works."

"We've got to be able to shut the net down! That's all there is to it!"

"And you'd then be the only ones who didn't have a way to check on what anyone else is doing. Even an old feasibility program half as sophisticated as mine would tell you that."

"How do we fight it?"

"By having someone who does understand it show you how to keep the information from being on the web in a usable form. Information carries its own tags, you know. You have to be able to avoid the tags and you can keep it secret for a little while."

"You can do that?"

"I haven't thought about it. I suppose so. It would be the best defense you could think of, really. I never thought about it much."

"When can you come to work? It will have to be where we can keep it secret!"

"Which would be a tag an idiot would find in about ten seconds. It doesn't get through to you that's exactly the thing that identifies a project?"

There was a whimper.

"I work at home. Nobody suspects a thing. I'm just cruising the forums and blogs, as always."

"But they wouldn't know that you weren't at home!" he cried triumphantly.

"Ever heard of an IPO?"

"Er?"

"Every time you go online there is a record. An IPO (He wasn't sure that was the right one, but this idiot certainly wouldn't!) is registered. It's international information. If some new one goes onto the forums it can be traced. An old one like mine is ignored."

"We don't have computers that get around that?"

"No. No registration, no use of the net. It's automatic and built into the machines. The best way to hide some kinds of things is the purloined letter."

"Is that some kind of program we can use?"

"You don't know what ... no. It's a psychological system. It works far more often than the best programs anyone can think up."

"Same salary? Five a month and expenses?"

"I ... well, okay. I can get by with that for a little while."

"You're on the clock as of now. Let me talk with our operative."

Phil handed Nort the phone.

What was that ... oh, shit! He ran into the house to find a big rat tranquilly eating the moldy bread on the kitchen counter. It had knocked a dish off onto the floor. He picked up a big knife and swung it at the rat. The rat dove off the counter and into the garbage pail. Phil slammed on the lid and took it outside.

He went back to tell Nort he would be getting to work

right away. Nort asked if he should stay around.

"Why?"

He shrugged. Phil said it would be a lot better if he didn't have visitors from the department. They were too easy to spot. He'd be watched. If it looked like he didn't accept the job they'd get tired of it after a day or two.

Nort left. He went out to the rat – that had gnawed a hole in the plastic garbage pail and escaped.

He went inside and cleaned up the kitchen. Now that drain was stopped up, but he knew that was back-pressure from the earlier toilet episode, so used the plunger. He then went to his computer to work for awhile, finding every project he could.

He then went to bed. Tomorrow would be something else! He wished he had a hint as to what.

Why Me, Lord?

One Year Later

Phil got out of bed and headed for the bathroom. He stepped into his slippers, one of which folded under. He almost fell, but caught the doorjamb. He cut himself slightly while he was shaving, then went into the kitchen to fix breakfast. He plugged in the coffee maker, which made a humming noise, then a pop.

He didn't pause. He took out a pan, dumped water in and coffee and sat it on the stove. He turned on the gas. There was a ball of fire that rose toward the ceiling a bit, then went out. Slow leak. He'd fixed it several times. He thought nothing of it. He rinsed the clean dishes in the drainer. He didn't doubt the rat had been in the house again. He wasn't about to take it outside if he got it again. It was a dead rat if he got it.

There was a knock on the door. He called that if they were there for God he'd see they got to him very fast. He'd told all of them not to come around anymore.

It was Gordon and Nort. They were going fishing. Did he want to come along? They were sort of pals. Gordon had confided after six months that he hadn't found two of the chickens. Both hens. It was long enough that the explosion thing was shown not to be passed on to any chicks and there hadn't been any exploding eggs they heard of. So long as no two of the chicks of those hens mated it was something in the past. Phil didn't try to explain skip-generation genetics. It probably wouldn't apply, anyhow.

"After last trip? When the trailer blew a tire, the motor never started, the plug came out and we almost sank? You would ask again?"

"It's really part of the job," Nort confided. "Don't let them know I told you that. They want to know how anyone can live with the constant crap your life is. It got to be a joke around the office. You came to the building twice and it almost burned down once and that bus went through the front door when the brakes failed the second time. They don't know how you can just go on like nothing happened."

"Oh, yeah. I hardly noticed. How is their program coming along?"

"Which one? You or the Flashlight Project?"

"That thing won't ever work. I gave them the facts about that. They ignored it. It wasn't what some bigshit scientist in Germany said. I showed them a few other things that ass said that were totally ridiculous.

"Come on in. Coffee should be ready."

He led them to the kitchen. They sat at the table. He got cups and a sock, strained the boiling coffee into the second pot, managed to spill some boiling water that barely missed going into his hand. When he pulled the hand away he managed to knock over the cooking oil that made a little puddle on the floor. He dropped some paper toweling on it and brought out the cream and sugar.

The cream was curdled. He dumped it into the sink and got some creamer in a jar. He turned to ask if they wanted some cinnamon rolls with the coffee, then banged his head on the cabinet door when he turned around again, not hard.

He poured his own cup and sat on the third chair. One leg collapsed, almost dumping him on the floor. He grabbed the fourth chair and sat in it, managing to dump over the creamer. Only a little spilled. Nort and Gordon were staring at him in disbelief. He didn't even seem to notice all the things that were happening.

He saw the looks. He grinned. "It's a little game God and I play. He tries to get a reaction, I refuse to react. It's just in fun ... I think."

He said there were some sticky buns in the other cabinet. He stood and opened the hanging cabinet door.

The rat jumped out almost into his face. He was finally fast enough to be able to swat it down. It was against the baseboard, scrambling to get to its feet. He smacked it with the frying pan. He got it by the tail and threw the lifeless body into the back yard.

"Pretty good one, Lord! I expected something such when I have guests. You'll have to get a new rat, I guess."

He washed his hands thoroughly and got the sticky buns. They were in a tin bread box, so the rat couldn't have gotten to them.

The three chatted awhile and ate the sticky buns. They still wanted to go fishing.

"Okay. We have a sort of agreement.

"Lord, how about a truce for the rest of the day? There's no reason for our little game to screw up the day for anyone else, like last time, okay?"

He got a sort of agreement feeling, but knew things would go on happening. They would only be things that didn't affect Nort and Gordon.

Like his reel with the wad of monofilament jamming it. Like the hooks on his favorite lure being rusted to where they would break if he got a big one. Like the reel oil leaking all over the tackle box. Like the artificial worms leaking smelly liquid in the box. Like his beer cooler lid snapping in two.

He shook his head and dropped the tackle box into the

trash can. He cut all the monofilament off the reel. They stopped at the shop where they launched the boat and Phil bought a lot of new stuff. What he'd made working for the government made it nothing.

"I see you bought stainless steel hooks this time," Nort noticed.

"I always do."

"But ... those were rusted you threw away!"

"Uh-huh. And?"

He shook his head. Phil slipped on the alga growing on the launch ramp, but caught onto the boat before he went down onto the concrete. His fishing hat blew off his head and got soaked.

Then they went out into the lake.

They were back at his house just before dark. He had a nice bass. He said there was always a consolation prize. He really did enjoy the game anymore.

He went into the kitchen when they left, still not quite believing the kinds of things that happened to Phil.

Phil managed to survive long enough to get to bed. In the morning he went out to his coop – he really did build a small one for his own use – and got a dozen eggs. He put ten of them in the refrigerator and took a bowl to make a two egg omelet. He tapped the eggs to crack them. The second one exploded.

"Good show, Lord! You really got me on that one! A point up for you!

"Used the old skip-generation thing and I've got a hen that lays the eggs.? I'm glad they didn't have the acrylic part yet.

"You wouldn't do anything that really would seriously

hurt me, would you?"

He cleaned up the mess.

Should he report this to the office?

No. It was a doomed trait. It would definitely be bred out of the chickens in the next generation.

Well! Things are normal! What should he do today?

$$"!"$$

$$"!"$$

Author's note:
This appeared in SSFSS2. It is based on a friend who is gay, who, unlike other gay friends, is ... much like Louie. He has read this little comic piece and thinks it's hilarious. He agrees that this could almost describe what would happen if....

$$"!"$$

Louie Turnbull stopped to peer cautiously into the thick brush lining the path to his right.

There was something there! He was positive!

So he wasn't much for the woodsy bit. He hadn't wanted to be included in this little outing in the first place. He liked city streets and discos with their punks and trade and prostitutes. He liked Margaritas in wide, flat, clean glasses on a slick plastic bar, not bitter coffee in dirty styrofoam cups on a rough log!

Trouble was, he liked Frank Ford even more.

Frank was tall, dark and slender, with almost-black eyes that made Louie weak in the knees.

Frank liked that Irene bitch who hung around Marty's Bar.

Irene liked anyone with fifty bucks.

There! That slithery sound that came from behind that wad of branches! There was a snake back there that was at least twice his size! He just KNEW it!

One thing Louie had learned on the streets of Chicago

was to face his fears and stare them down. Otherwise, they would become bigger and stronger than he was.

Of course, if there was some huge boa constrictor in there he could be crushed to death before he had a chance to move! Louie liked the erotic symbolism. Crushed to death by some monster phallic symbol.

He wouldn't get such a big thrill from the reality, no doubt.

Very carefully and timidly, Louie crept stealthily and watchfully around the thickly-woven branches of the juvenile cedar. There was nothing there. Just more bushes and rocks and a sort of little cleft in the side of a low hill with a pebbly stream beside it..

He sighed, rolled his eyes and started to move on, then he heard what he was sure was someone swearing in a foreign language. (You know how easy it is to tell when someone's swearing, no matter that the words don't make sense?) It was coming from the little cave in the hill.

Louie was suddenly curious. It might be some hermit or whacko, but there couldn't be anybody more nutty than the people he ran around with every day. He could handle that!

He went to stare into the darkness. He couldn't see a thing, but could smell a bit of sulfur. There was a little thumping sound and a single explosive exclamation.

"Hoo-hooo! Anybody home?" Louie called. "Come out, come out, whoever you are!"

There was a sudden ominous silence. Even the infernal buzzing and chirping of bugs and birds stopped.

Maybe that was natural out here. How would HE know?

"Yooo-hooo!" he called, starting to move into the cleft as his eyes adjusted to the pitch-black darkness inside. He had to bend over at the entrance, but the cave quickly expanded to become a large open bubble. There was a small fire across the space, maybe sixty feet away. Louie could soon begin to make out details. He couldn't see anyone, but he could feel eyes watching him. It was eerie and sort of exciting.

He excited very easily.

A sort of blacker blackness moved between him and the fire. It was about seven feet tall and seemed to move in a smooth flowing fashion – like a dancer or athlete, Louie decided.

"You really should get more light in here," Louie chided. "You'll get eyestrain.

"I'm Louie, but my friends call me Louise.

"What's your name? What're you doing out here in this godforsaken *hole*?"

The shape moved to add a lot of smaller branches to the fire, causing it to quickly grow. He could soon see.

Well! *That* was a shocker!

Louie, frozen to the spot, looked over his ... host. He was afraid he'd faint, at first, but managed not to.

The ... guy ... was about seven feet tall, was covered in shiny black fur, had big pointed ears and little horns, slanted, slit-pupilled eyes and long fangs. And a tail. And hooves instead of toes. And claws instead of fingernails.

He was certainly muscular, with a massive chest, and such *big* biceps, and a little waist, and powerful thighs – and he was most very *definitely* male!

Louie was still scared, but he was also excited and more than a little interested!

"I am Astoreth, elemental lord of dark regions!"

"Ooooohh! You have a mag*nifi*cent speaking voice!"

Louie gushed.

"Huh?" Astoreth replied. "You may find your final fate here, mortal!"

"I can think of a few ways that could most *certainly* be made *very* pleasant!" Louie rejoined, staring at Astoreth's crotch. "You certainly are a *big* one, aren't you? I'll bet a girl would never forget a tumble with *you*!"

"Huh?" Astoreth replied, brightly.

"Don't you have a more comfortable place than all these hard rocks?" Louie asked, coyly. "Not that I object to *hard* at all!

"Oooh! I'm just *aw*ful, but I find you *most* attractive! Sex on the hoof! Literally! I just *love* it!"

"Yeeesh!" Astoreth replied, backing away.

"Don't be so shy! We're all alone with nature here and I'd sure like to get to know more about *your* nature, Nature Boy! Oh, yes indeedy!" Louie said as he started moving toward Astoreth. "Damned laced pants! Always a knot at the *worst* possible time!"

Astoreth backed toward the wall – and kept on backing until he was completely gone. Louie stared uncomprehending at the spot for a minute, sighed, and said, "I guess I came on a little strong for the country scene, hunh?"

He sighed again, relaced his pants and went back to camp, where Frank greeted him with, "I met this really hot chick over at the west campsite! I even got lucky! How about you?"

"I don't like the woodsy scene," Louie pouted. "I'm for city people and city places. I can't *understand* anybody out here!

"I met a really nice guy, but he was too shy to make it. There are some interesting characters, but I just do not stand a prayer of *understanding* them!

"I'm getting awfully frustrated, Frank. How about...?"

"Louie, I've told you a million times before, I like you and all, but it isn't my thing," Frank said, patiently. "Just friends is as far as it will ever go. Sex is *out*!"

Louie sighed. The guy back there wouldn't even go *that* far!

He couldn't wait to get back to Chi. They didn't do one single *thing* out here like back in the city. He would simply never be able to *undrstand* these weird country people!

What a Weekend!
© 2015 by C. D. Moulton

Experiences with going to forums and groups on such as Facebook gave me ideas for this one. If you are a member of any of the types of groups where this kind of people are major contributors, perhaps you will see yourself (Hah! Get real!) as others see you. I reserve a few paragraphs here and there to soapbox on issues. It's called artistic license (like anyone could get a license for THAT!) and I don't pretend any different. I try not to lie to myself. I'm not always successful in that endeavor.

Resemblances to personalities of groups is synthesized from those groups encountered on Face Book and such sites.

Contents

Trip to the Store

Well! That was a bit unexpected!

Manny Grantley sighed and pulled into the parking lot at Super-Fine Everything Stores to drift to a stop. It was late and there were no other cars this far from the entrance to the store.

MG, as his friends called him, got out of the new Frevy and opened the hood.

He didn't know squat about cars. There was a lot of smoke coming from down on the left side. Other than that, nothing he could see.

The damned thing didn't have a hundred miles on it! What could go wrong with a new thirty thousand dollar car in four days? It had to happen on Friday night on top of that?

If he'd had a date he'd be royally pissed. As it was, he was only pissed.

The parking lot cop pulled to beside him to lean out the window and say he had to move into a slot. He wasn't allowed to block the drive.

"It quit on me. That's why the hood's open. I can't move it, and what is it blocking? There's an acre of flat pavement here with nothing on it!"

"You have to stop in a slot or you will be towed!" the cop returned.

"Okay. Car! Start and pull into a slot! That is an order!"

The cop stared at him.

"Gee! It didn't do what I ordered!"

"Move it or it gets towed!"

"Okay. It will have to get towed anyway. It, if it didn't

register the first time, quit on me. That's why it's sitting here *with the hood up.*"

"I'm not here to argue with you! Move it or it gets towed!"

"I just said you can have it towed."

"Why are you being so obstinate? I never did anything to you! Move it or it gets towed."

"Fuck you."

"That did it! You're under arrest!"

"Fuck you. You can't arrest anyone. You're a make-believe cop on a private parking lot. Christ!"

"I mean it! Move it or I call the cops!"

"I just said you should do that. Call them. Call the tow truck."

The barely more than teenage cop looked uncertain. He picked up his walky-talky and said he needed help. MG could hear the answer.

"What are you into now, Donny? You'd better not have screwed up another one! Mrs. Ames is still giving us hell because of that! Roberts is threatening to sue! What now?"

"This guy is parked right in the middle of the entrance lane! He's blocking the lane! He won't move!"

"Let me talk to him."

"I told him we would have it towed and he said, 'Fuck you,' and that ain't right!"

"Let me talk to him."

"I mean, like, he refuses to do what I say and he doesn't respect my authority! He won't move and he's blocking the entrance lane!"

"Donny, let me talk to him, right now! I don't care if your uncle owns the place, you just work, HAH! for it. Put him on!"

"I only said…"

"PUT HIM ON!"

"But he's blocking the lane!"

"It's eleven thirty and they can drive a hundred feet away to get around him! PUT HIM ON!"

"But they would have to go outside the lane marks!"

"PUT HIM ON! **NOW**! YOU FUCKING IDIOT!"

"You don't have to get abusive." He handed MG the radio just as a delivery truck came in and passed about sixty feet away. The idiot cop waved at it. MG shrugged and put a hand up. The cop looked more sullen.

"I'm on. What the hell is happening?"

"I'm sorry, sir. New trainee, relative of the owner. What's going on?"

"My car quit just as I was turning in. I don't know what's wrong. It's a new car. I looked in under the hood, but I don't know anything about mechanics. This turkey comes up and starts ranting about moving it to a slot."

"The hood's open?!" MG could hear the disbelief in the voice.

"Uh-huh. And a damned big truck just went through without coming even close, so I'm not blocking anything."

"I'm sorry about this, sir. We will have aid sent to you immediately. Our customers are important to us. We know these things happen.

"Will you put Donny on, please?"

MG handed the radio to a sullen pouting Donny.

"Yeah. What?"

"You will either repair the client's car, personally, or you will call a service for him. We will pay all costs and you will apologize to the gentlemen sincerely. You will wait for the repair service, then will come directly to the office.

Is that clear?"

"I don't see why I have to..."

"IT WASN'T A REQUEST YOU GODDAMNED MORON! IT WAS AN ORDER!"

"I ain't gonna call no repair for some guy who won't respect my authority!"

"YOU DON'T HAVE ANY DAMNED AUTHORITY, you hair-brained fucking half-assed idiot! CALL ... no. I will. You will come to the office, NOW! You are relieved of duty indefinitely."

"You can't do that!"

"Yes, I can. I just did. Put the gentleman on again."

"I ain't gonna...."

"PUT HIM ON OR I'M GOING TO COME OUT THERE AND PERSONALLY KICK YOUR SORRY SNIVELING FUCKING ASS TO THE CORNER AND BACK!"

Donny sullenly handed the radio to MG.

"I've gone into deep hallucinations, haven't I?" MG said. "This has to be a sick joke or something. I'm on Candid Camera or something, aren't I?"

"God! I wish!"

"What kind of car are you driving, sir?"

"Frevy Elite."

"What year ... sorry. Elite is this year."

"Yeah. Doesn't have a hundred miles on it yet."

"Well, the dealership is four blocks away and they have all night repair service. It will be under warranty, so won't cost anything. As soon as they get here, come to the office for your gift certificate."

"Gift certificate?"

"Yeah. Donny-boy just bought you a hundred dollar gift

certificate for the time and aggravation."

"I *what*?! I ain't bought nobody nothing!" Donny yelled.

"Sure, you did! It will be taken out of your severance pay. Argue with me and it's a five hundred dollar certificate, got it?"

Donny grabbed the radio out of MG's hand and got in the car, slammed the door, and drove off toward the building.

MG was standing there, mouth hanging open in disbelief. This couldn't be real! He got the giggles. He knew, from his use of Facebook, that some people really were that stupid. They got an idea in their heads and you couldn't make them see reality with an H-bomb.

After about twenty minutes the Frevy repair truck showed up. A hairy overweight man got out and took a box from in back of the truck and a toolbox. He said it would take about half an hour. The starter jammed on that model and burned out, making the electrical system shut down.

MG started to say something, then said he was going to the store and would be back out in a few minutes.

What he walked into in the office was no more real to him than what had happened on the parking lot.

What the Hell...?

"Sir, I am Charlie Burns. I'm security manager. I want to apologize for the way our rookie guard acted. It is *not* the way he was trained to relate to people."

"Manny Grantley. MG. I couldn't believe ... he's sitting out there giving me dirty looks. What's up with him?"

"His uncle, Frank Cutter, owns the place. We were to cut him slack at first, but this time exceeded the rules. His father and uncle will be here in a few minutes."

"I can see how he couldn't get a job anywhere else. Is he really retarded to that extent?"

"Wait 'til you meet ... I'd better shut up. I need this job."

"Understood. I'll hang around to back you up if you like."

Donny stomped into the room and demanded to know what MG was lying about with what happened when he refused to obey an order from a policeman.

"What policeman?!" MG asked.

"Me!"

"You aren't a policeman. You're a damned private security guard," MG pointed out.

"*Was*," Charlie corrected.

"You'll get yours when my Pops gets here! You can't get away with setting me up like this. It's all a lie! I just asked him to move the car and he wouldn't! Nothing else! It's all a lie to set me up!"

"Everything on the walky-talky is recorded," Charlie said dryly.

"YEEP!"

A big black car pulled up to the loading dock and two

all lies!"

"It's a recording, you half-assed idiot!" Charlie returned.

"Now, now," Pops cried. "Let's chill out for a bit and see what really happened!"

"This is not happening!" MG said, shaking his head. "There are no such things as these people! I'm just hallucinating! I have to be! *This cannot be happening*!"

"I agree with you, Sir," Charlie said.

"Now, now," Pops cried, giving Donny a withering look. "This will blow over. If Mr. ... er, the man, er, uh, will kindly sign the release we will handle it."

Charlie winked and shook his head the least bit.

"I won't sign anything without my lawyer here," MG replied. He saw what Charlie was doing. Make them think he was going to sue them.

"I'm suppose Mr. ... er, knows it was just a little incident that got out of hands because neither side would give a little bit," the boss wheedled.

"WHAT?!?!" MG yelled. "I was stopped with the *hood* up because the car quit *right there*! This ... thug in a uniform made ridiculous demands and *humiliated* me in public for *no reason whatever* than to make himself look like a bigshot is a *little incident*!?!"

"Er, uh, Sir!" from the boss.

"Now, now!" from Pops.

A grin from Charlie.

"Sir, may I speak to you in private?" Charlie asked, with a big wink at the boss. "I'm sure we can work out something to mutual advantage."

"You're nothing but a fucking jerk who wants to get me fired!" Donny cried.

Pops smacked him so hard he hit the floor. "I've had

enough of you and your shit mouth! I don't care what your mother says, no more! I'll whup your slimy sorry worthless ass from here to sundown! No more! You keep me broke now, you little jackass cowflop!

"Charlie, you're right! You were all along! You always said he's a worthless piece of shit who hides behind his mother's skirts! I've had to get him out of trouble fifty times! NO MORE! Nah-ahnh! NO FUCKING MORE!" he turned to Donny, who was crying.

"You get another place to stay! You straighten up and grow up or you can starve in the street! ENOUGH, ALREADY!

"How did such a wonderful person as your mother raise a piece if *shit* like you? There's never been any such thing on my side of the family! I never knew about anything on *her* side, so where did you get it, you sniveling little pig turd? I should have taken over ten years ago and maybe you'd be worth trying to change."

"Hah!" Donny said with a sneer. "I ain't your kid! Mom told me that three years ago! That's why I don't look none like you an your ... UH! I mean, uh..."

"What!? She said ... *what*!?"

"EEEEP! I mean, like I didn't say what ... she only said I didn't *act* like I was your kid. Oh, shit!"

"She WHAT!?"

"Pops! I didn't mean it!"

"Don't you never call me 'Pops' again or I'll break your sorry sniveling ass in two! I'll *kill* that bitch!"

"Pops! I ... oh, God!"

Pops slammed out the door.

"You'd better call Irene and warn her," Charlie said to the boss.

"I'll talk to you tomorrow," MG said. He waved and went out.

He had to be hallucinating. He had to be! This couldn't be real! It simply couldn't! *No* one could be ... like that! A whole family of them?

He went out to get his car.

It wasn't there.

What now?

He called the agency. The woman who answered said the car was repaired. The repairman said he would come out for it in a few minutes and had returned to the agency. Would MG please come in to sign the repair ticket for the insurance company?

"You have my car there?"

"Er, a moment."

He waited. She came back on to say the repairman left the car there.

"It's not here now. Did he leave the keys in the car?"

"A moment." Another thirty seconds. "Yes. You couldn't drive it without the keys. They are in the ignition, if you will look."

"I would love to look, but the car is gone.

"Your repairman left the keys to a new thirty thousand dollar car, sitting a long way from any other cars on a virtually empty parking lot in a less than minimal security, in the ignition and just drove away?"

"Er, that is."

"You will deliver me a car of equal or more value within ten minutes and will replace the items I had inside. I'll be right here. You get your car back when I have mine back and in new condition, plus a hundred bucks a mile for anything other than the mileage on the receipt."

"We can't do that, Sir!"

"Then I'll sue the piss out of you, take over the agency and fire some incompetent ass who would leave the keys etc. Got it?"

"Er, that is."

"You said that."

The line went dead.

What the hell was happening!? Had he slipped into some weird alternate universe or something?

He sighed and looked at the sign over the entrance. "God is all. Put your trust in the Lord and your future will be bright".

Oh, whoopie! Problems solved! And it was so easy!

No car came, so he went to the agency. They were open until twelve, which was nine minutes from now. He was going to make it a memorial six or seven when he got there. Repair was open all night.

The office was closed.

The repair dispatcher said there was some kind of emergency, so they closed ten minutes early. It didn't matter because no one would come that time of night, anyhow.

"I'm here, in case you didn't notice."

"You shouldn't wait so late for that kind of thing."

"What kind of thing?"

"What?"

"You said I shouldn't come so late because of that kind of thing. What kind of thing?"

"Whatever kind of thing. You should come earlier."

"Well, I would, except the car I bought four days ago broke down at this hour. You should arrange for them to break down at a better time."

Was this kind of thing going to go on and on?

"That new? What model?"

"Elite."

"Oh. Yeah. Starter burned out?"

"Seems expected."

"Yeah. Mold on the tranny plate was cast at an angle and it burns them out."

"And you just go on selling them without warning the customer?"

"Well, *I* don't. I run repair. They're going to replace all the bad plates when the new ones are delivered."

"I don't believe this! What does that mean?"

"The Casting and Forms Union's on strike and they can't get anything done. They have to catch up. Same as here. Scabs don't do so good a job."

"They don't do as good as the regular union bunch who screwed it up in the first place?"

"Not my problem. Got the same problem here. Special Repair Service and Boiler Attendant's Society is on strike and we're using scabs. It ... oh. Elite starter. Fred Jobes. He put on a R-two, so it should last a few months. They'll have the new plates by then. He left the receipt here for the insurance, so I guess you came to sign it."

"No. I came to get a replacement car. The idiot left the keys in the ignition and came back here while I was in the store. The car was stolen because of his neglect. I want a replacement until they locate my car."

"Well, the office would have to handle that, but they're closed."

"You finally got it!"

"I can't do anything. There's nothing in the book about me doing that."

"The book?"

"Yeah. We have a rule book and we can't do anything unless it's in the book. The office has their book. It's supposed to be the same, but mine doesn't have the old section that says what to do when their rules don't fit what we have. Or like that."

"So I'm supposed to do what? Walk? Because your representative got my car stolen and your office is closed?"

"It'll open Monday morning at nine."

"And?"

He shrugged. "Not my problem. It's not in my book, so I'm supposed to act like it don't exist."

"What am I supposed to do?"

"Well, the bus. There's a twenty four hour Hertz at the airport. You could rent a car. Budget's cheaper, but they don't have as good cars. Taxis cost too much anymore."

MG was talking to another idiot. He couldn't believe this was happening! He had to be dreaming or hallucinating! This kind of thing couldn't be happening!

He controlled his urge to yank this moron over the counter and smash his stupid face in. He turned and walked out without another word.

The idiot called that he would leave a note for the office that he came in and lodged a complaint that was their problem, not his.

He hailed a taxi (that smelled like a sick drunk had just used it) and went home. He was lucky, in that he didn't have plans for tomorrow – today, actually – or Sunday that would mean he needed the car. He rode buses for four years before buying that piece of professionally designed shit, which had him prepared to live with the designer's fuck-ups.

Why in all the imaginable hells would they use a, what did he call it? Starter plate ... no. Tranny plate. A tranny plate they knew was defective? Why would they just leave it there?

Welcome to the orderly universe and corporate business methods. Things are normal.

He still couldn't believe this was happening. He knew about programmed people from the news. Was everybody in this town programmed somehow to act like defective robots?

He went in and started to get ready for bed. Nothing else to do. He cleaned up and showered, knew he wouldn't sleep in this mood, so decided to watch TV. He went to the programs. The thoughts of a few minutes ago came to mind. Programmed.

A list of movies. *Fast and Furious* number one through however many they had now. *Star Wars*, all episodes. Old reruns of the Sparta and Trojan Wars, Pirates of the Caribbean, a glut of those ridiculous vampire and zombie crap ... a bunch of karate and tae-kwan-do crap ... those Conan things ... drug lords and drug cops blowing up everything in sight and machine gunning a few million windows. Armored cars going up a ramp and running into a helicopter, resulting in an explosion that would make Bikini look like a firecracker? Stuff from the serial killer craze.

Everything on most of them were war and mayhem overdone special effect crap. Wrestling, where they ran amok and hit each other over the head with chairs and such, where blows and kicks that would kill if they were real, yet not a mark on anyone after the match?

Everything was glorified violence and murder.

Other types. Forest Gump. An idiot who came out looking smarter than ... and he was wondering how the programming was accomplished? Well, DUH!

Nature. Sharks and tigers killing gazelles and polar bears killing seals and salmon and snakes killing rats and crocodiles killing racoons and eagles killing other birds and small animals and even fish. Stars going supernova. Tornadoes destroying houses. Carnivorous plants. All shown in gory detail and close-up.

Science. The development of nuclear weapons. How genetic manipulation could make a race of docile slaves or an army of super soldiers.

He went to children's programming. He didn't at all like what he was thinking.

All karate and monsters and transformers made to look cute while they rampaged through the world..

He felt really sick. Why hadn't he seen this when he was ten years old? It was that obvious!

Because it had worked on him until ... now. It finally became too extreme for him not to see what was going on. He and everyone else were being programmed since birth.

Who? Why?

Why was easy enough. Money and power.

Who? Back when he was just able to understand words at all?

"Jesus loves me this I *know*, for the *Bible* tells me so!" Stress that you *know* it because it's in the *Bible*. Three years old, and programmed while the mind was just beginning information storage and processing. No wonder there were so many obnoxious evangelicals running around!

Grammar school. Act like *this* because it's what *good*

people do and what the big *stars* say to do and what those generals who *saved* you from the *horror* of what some other general who worked for another political view would cause.

I'm programmed enough that I'll just note it and move on.

He went to bed. He didn't sleep well.

What a Weekend!

Saturday in Hell

MG caught the early bus into town. Luckily, the stop was right out his front gate. He didn't have much to do, so would go back home for the afternoon. It was fairly early, so wouldn't be crowded. His luck had always been that some fat woman with a perspiration problem would wiggle in next to him and try to flirt. Or a preacher out to save the world from itself.

Door number two today.

"What a delightful bright and sunny morning, Brother! The Lord has blessed this day and has given us a gift of beauty and peace!!"

"Not for me."

"Oh? Tell me your problems, my child! I'm *certain* the Lord, with my help, will solve all evils and lead you to glory! Peace and plenty is here for all who will but accept that he is our lord and savior."

"I doubt it."

"And why would you doubt what is promised in the Holy Scriptures, the direct word of the Lord as dictated to those fine and loyal men who placed their lives into his charge? You have doubts? I can, with God's help, sweep those problems out of your life!"

"Well, the main one at the moment, you could solve very easily."

"Ah! And that is? I am here to serve the Lord, who works through pitiful undeserving me to save the fallen and those in doubt of the truth of his word! Amen!"

"You. I don't believe that crap. You will sit there and try to convince me of three impossible things before lunch.

You could solve that problem by simply moving to any one of a dozen empty seats on this bus."

"But, my dear Brother! I am called by the Lord God to save your immortal soul from the clutches of Satan's evil domain!"

"I'll have to Google that domain. Would it be satansevil dot com?"

"You would mock the Lord in such a way? You are *damned*! Your eternal soul will burn in the fires of *Hell!* I declare it!"

"Doesn't your god reserve the right of judgement? Wouldn't you be the one damned if you try to usurp the things he has reserved for himself, alone? Are you one of those who think your scriptural instructions apply to others, not to you?"

"I will not hear Satan's twisted mouthings from such as you! I will not hear your evil contortions of the Holy Scriptures, dictated in certain truth by the Lord God, himself! I will not hear it! The spirit of Satan speaks through you in his forked tongue! I do not – I WILL not hear you!

"Why would anyone try to change a serious devout person's beliefs? You, Sir, are among the *damned*! Death to the heretics!"

"Isn't your loving and compassionate god a little strong on 'kill this or that person if they will not crawl around my mythical feet?' You're still usurping you god's right to be the sole judge. Naughty! Naughty!"

"I don't know how to get through to one who has so deeply fallen. Perhaps my method is a bit too far, for which I deeply and sincerely apologize. In truth, I fear for the fate of your immortal soul. I may be moved to excess, but the surrendering of the self to evil … it is what has happened to this sad world since it strayed from the path."

"That would make a good rap number! I Fear for the Fate of your Farty Hole!"

"You, Sir, are unable to accept the truth! I speak for truth! I know the absolute truth that you refuse to see, though it is plainly shown in every beautiful sunrise, in every lovely flower, in every wonderful, beautiful butterfly! In the lovely fishes of the sea"

"Well, yesterday it was raining at sunrise. I have a couple of plants in my lawn with flowers that are as ugly as homemade sin and the caterpillars are not exactly exquisite. I don't think you or anyone else can say that a dogfish is lovely. You spout that crap in your stentorian tones with the deepest conviction. You aim for the truth, you claim. You will impress me with that truth, no matter how much you have to lie to reach that height."

"You are incorrigible!"

"I tried to tell you that from the first. Here comes my stop. Have a nice day irritating people. I guess that's your basic goal. You just want to impress people with the strength of your weird beliefs.

"You do make a strong impression! I'll certainly give you that!"

"Why, thank you, Sir! It is most kind of you to understand that. I *do* represent the Lord God!"

"Too bad that's the opposite of what you impressed them with, huh? Bye!"

Today, so far, was typical. MG wondered if that would continue. He considered the night before and felt a small tingling of dread that it would return, that it wasn't just some kind of crazy nightmare.

He decided he would stop in the police station, just down the block, to report his stolen car. The insurance would require that, and the agency office wouldn't open before nine on Monday, so they wouldn't report it, for sure.

He handled that. A super-efficient desk sergeant took his statement and put out an immediate APB for the car. If it was located CSI was to be called immediately. MG would be notified.

He went to Home Depot for some electrical things he needed to make repairs in his apartment, then went to Henry's for some new socks and underwear, then to Mini*Plus for some spices and meat, then home. This time, seeing he had two big sacks of groceries and a small one of fittings, he got door number one. A fat sweaty woman in her fifties or early sixties who was trying to be coy and clever while batting overly made up eyes at him. He knew how to handle that one!

He went into a minor coughing fit, then apologized. "Flu going around, you know."

She suddenly wanted a seat on the other side four rows back.

He puttered around the apartment for a couple of hours, then went to Andy's Nuthouse, a local pub, for a cold beer and to watch the Yankees game. He was just leaving when two policemen – well, a police man and a police woman – came to look over the patrons. The woman asked Andy something, then came over, moving to one side of him while the man moved to the other. She suddenly yelled, "NOW!" and drew her Glock to point at him. The police man pointed his own at him.

"Manuel Markus Gravely, you are under arrest! Do not try to resist! You have the right to remain silent! Anything you say can be used against you in a court of law! You have the right to an attorney. If you cannot afford one, the court will appoint one. Do you understand these rights?"

"Que?" MG answered. This could *not* be happening!

She looked uncertain. She put the pistol back in its holster and asked the man if he understood Spanish. No.

"Uh, that is, would someone tell him what I said?"

"I speak English," MG said. "You were just so comical I couldn't resist.

"What would you have done if I didn't speak English?"

She giggled. "Good one! To tell the truth, I don't have a hint. Probably cuff you and take you in, but I wouldn't worry about the Miranda thing because I couldn't repeat whatever you said, anyhow."

"Can you tell me what I've supposedly done to result in an arrest like I was some dangerous international spy or an ax murderer or something?"

"A stolen car?"

"So my car was stolen. What in hell has that got to do with the Gangbusters bit?"

"Your car? There is a report of a stolen vehicle, class B, new ... Frevy Elite. Stolen from a parking lot last night. It was found parked at a bar on Seventh Street. Your prints were all over it. We have prints from your driver's license, you know."

"And?"

"*Stolen* car? *Your* prints?"

"It's my car. Why wouldn't my prints be all over it?"

She turned to the radio on a strap on her shoulder.

"Could your buddy point that thing somewhere else?" MG asked. She waved to him and he holstered the Glock. She said, "Report SV RCVD Seventh bar. Prints ID'ed M.

Gravely. OOR?"

"Manuel Markus Gravely. Male. Twenty eight years. Five eleven, one eighty. MM. Brown, brown, NDM. Two thirty nine B Elm Street. NOW."

"I have an order to arrest Gravely because his prints were found in the car. I did. Now what?"

There was a silence for awhile. MG asked, "I got everything but the OOR. What's that?"

"Owner of Record."

The radio came on to tell her to bring Gravely in. There were traces of cocaine found in the car. In the driver's seat.

"Let's see. A stolen car recovered in front of a bar on skid row that had traces of cocaine in the driver's seat is reason to arrest the car's owner for auto theft?" MG asked.

"Er, that is."

"Now who said that to me, just last night?"

"I don't know what you're talking about. Just come to the station with the officer and we can straighten it out."

"Okay. I can pick up the car."

"No. It has been confiscated. It was used in the drug trade."

"SAY WHAT!?"

"Sir, traces of cocaine were found inside the car!"

"Traces in a stolen car on the driver's seat is evidence of drug dealing from the car? *Traces*? Isn't there some kind of thing about quantity in that law?"

"Er, that is."

"Deja vu."

"What?"

"I'll come in. I will claim my car. If you keep it, you will get some of the kind of publicity several other police departments are enjoying on the news lately."

"Sir, it is not the police who confiscate property, it is the court. The federal court."

"We'll argue that in a less public venue, if you will be so kind. I have been publicly humiliated for the second time in two days. I'm getting damned sick and tired of it."

"Er, yes. Do that."

He waved for the cops to lead on. They went out and he got in the back, joking with the woman while the man looked sullen and mad as hell.

"What's the matter with him?" MG asked.

"Oh, he's too serious. He thinks police don't screw up, no matter how many times we do. We're just human, for Christ's sake!"

"I could teach you a lot about who screws up. I speak from experience!"

"Yeah. I can guess. To tell you the truth, Eddie there would like an excuse to shoot you. you're black and – Mexican?"

"Uh-huh. I'm an American. I think a few cops are exactly what they look like to the radical black community. I also think it's stupid beyond belief what those who call everybody black a thug and criminal or everybody who's white a slaveholder mentality or every Chinese a secret tong enforcer or everybody who looks a little Arabic a terrorist or everybody Jewish a Zionist are certifiable anti-social idiots. My great grandmother was Jewish, so my mother was, so I am. I'm also Irish, Latino, Lebanese, black. I guess I'm a mixture of the worst traits of all of them.

"Funny. I don't give a damn about money, drink very little, speak truly horrible Spanish, think terrorists and their backers should be blown off the planet's face, and don't hold anyone responsible for what their grandparents did, and think those two ignorant black bitches who are all over the net walking on our flag should have the holy living hell stomped out of them and then get deported to Nigeria or Ghana or wherever they think is so wonderful.

"I'm a misfit all around."

They pulled into the police station and got out. Eddie McVee took the car around to the lot and Anna Blevins and MG went into the station to vehicular, where an FBI agent was waiting. They had a radio receiver on the desk.

"I think Eddie is sorry he left the thing on so we could hear you. I'm Agent Cummins, FBI."

"I'm MG Gravely, general bum and human being."

Cummins laughed. "We were trying to link the bar where your car was found with a major drug supplier. The theory was that you arranged a transfer, it was taken in your car to the bar for delivery, then you would get the car back and a few hundred G's for your trouble. Your little speech in the police car sort of shot that one down big time."

"You used a radio in my car to spy on what we were doing without my knowledge?" Anna asked sweetly. "Warrant, please."

"It's a police vehicle. You have to assume there is always a tap in it," MG said.

"Yes. This state. Not FBI," she fired back.

"They aren't as bad as their reputation, either," MG said.

Cummins laughed.

"Usually."

He really laughed, then. Anna giggled and agreed.

"You get your car back, good as new," Cummins said. "We never completed the confiscation certificate. It was falling apart before we got that far."

"Whoopie! I get it back, good as new? With a tranny plate designed so badly it burns out the starter in less than four days. Thanks heaps!"

He remembered something, then. "Cummins, was the place my car was stolen from part of your equation!"

"Uh-huh. There's a connection. We can't figure it. If it wasn't for that, we wouldn't have even known about the car."

"Maybe I can't figure it, either. I might have a little bit of an answer to a question I've asked myself – lie! It didn't occur to me until just now! I wondered how a certain group of people could actually exist. They could if they were stoned out of their gourds. It could be because they fell into the trap of using their own product."

"Using their own product? Hooked on coke?"

"A crackhead would explain one of them. Lines would explain another. Add them together and you get a situation that can make you think you've fallen into an alternate reality. They would be damned easy to control if they were addicted and could have the supply cut off if they don't, shall we say, cooperate."

"That will take some explanation. That will take a *lot* of explanation!"

"I suppose you can get some information. We can make a plan. I'm in a position to bring a little pressure in one place."

"I don't have a clue as to what you're talking about!"

"Distraction."

"Distraction?"

"Distraction. What was going on while that silly staged farce was going down? Do you have someone watching the place who would concentrate on that while something else was happening right under their nose?"

Cummins looked thoughtful. "Could be. Just could be!

"Hint?"

"How many delivery trucks go to that place at eleven thirty on a Friday night?"

Cummins registered shock. "I'll be damned!"

"You'll have company."

"What?"

"Never mind."

A Little Logic

MG got out of his car at the entrance to Super Fine Everything store. Cummins (nobody ever calls me anything else, except maybe "Asshole") got out of the passenger side. They went in the main entrance to find Donny standing there in uniform.

That *did* get to MG.

"You weren't fired?!" MG asked.

"I ain't got nothin' to say to you!"

MG shook his head and went toward the office. Cummins asked, "He the guard you told me about?"

"Uh-huh."

"You were serious? That shit really went down?"

"Uh-huh."

"I think I'm beginning to believe you really do have this figured out."

"A little logic: why else would he still be here? I was the third such distraction in three weeks. A delivery truck at almost midnight."

"But ... where it fails is why you were there. That had to be an accidental thing, your car breaking down at just that time and place?"

"He would have done something to draw attention if I wasn't there. He was in that car, driving around, looking for anything. I guess he would have created a diversion some way. Maybe run into a car or something."

They went into the hall and back to the loading dock and security office. Charlie was there. He was a little flabbergasted when MG walked in.

"Er, Mr. Gravely, was it? Is there a problem?"

"Lot of them, but there always are. I just decided to sue this place off the map. I was just going to ask if you would have the recording copied for me, but walked in the front entrance door and dear, dear, Donny-boy was standing right there in uniform!"

"His uncle owns the place. What can I say?"

"His uncle owns a place that is going to be sued because of his actions in three cases, exactly one week apart?" Cummins asked. "Isn't that even further out than the little theatrics bit last night?"

"Er, theatrics?"

"Good cop, bad cop theatrics. Just a little different definition of cops. Once, probably just an idiot employee, though the employee would definitely be fired. Second time, possible, but very highly unlikely coincidence. Third time, it's pure bullshit. Add that it was between eleven and twelve o'clock PM on consecutive Friday nights and you could be more subtle with a hundred foot flashing neon and halogen billboard."

"But ... what would be the object? This doesn't make sense!"

"I just can't figure how my car ... I'll be damned!" MG exclaimed. "Cummins, who else left prints in my car?"

"Prints? I don't ... let me check." He called the CSI department and asked about prints found at crime scene twelve forty one SVR. After about three uncomfortable minutes, he said, "Seven sets, five identified, two not. None on the steering wheel. It was wiped. It and the gearshift knob.

"You got a candidate for the unidentified prints? Will it mean anything?" he asked MG.

"It'll mean someone has to explain the prints being there.

Someone who hasn't got a chance of explaining why his prints are there."

"Who?"

"I believe his name's Cutter?"

Charlie groaned. "I refuse to answer any questions not asked in the presence of my attorney."

"Cutter? The owner?" Cummins asked.

"The prints, his brother, Papa ... well, he thought so. That may have been real ... of the lovely Donny Cutter, security officer standing right out front."

"Because?"

"He ran out of here because Donny had just made a slip that he wasn't actually his father. When I went out a few minutes later, the car that he came in was still sitting by the loading dock. Mine was gone."

Cummins' cellular buzzed. He answered, listened for a minute, then put it back in his pocket..

"George Yancy Cutter? His prints are on file for a firearms permit."

MG raised an eyebrow at Charlie, who nodded.

"Well, we have the in. Now we find a little bit of proof and this one's a done case," Cummins said.

"Well, the stuff was delivered in a pretty good-sized truck. What could have been taken out in my car wasn't much. That means it will be around here somewhere."

"The dogs couldn't find it."

"They try the freezers?"

"Yeah. Want to look around a bit when the crew gets here to have a little talk with Donny and Charlie et al?"

"What would I see that you didn't?"

"Maybe something like a question of what was being delivered under our noses at midnight?"

"There's that. I don't have anything else to do."

"A deal?" Charlie asked.

"What?" from Cummins.

"For a little consideration, such as that I was forced into this ...?"

"How?"

"A close relative is in a position to end up dead. You'll have to protect him as part of the deal."

"Okay, if it's true and if your information proves out."

Cummins' phone buzzed. He answered and went out to return with four uniformed police and a fellow agent. And Donny, who was really crying this time.

Charlie was led out. Donny saw him being treated a little roughly. He would tell the others that.

They went back to the freezers. Charlie said maybe they should check if the light switches were all working, that maybe the three that didn't seem to be in use were to all be turned on at once with the thermostat turned up to fifty three degrees F?

A small section in the back wall slid open. There were bales stacked to the top and several black plastic boxes stacked to one side. Cummins checked the bales first, announced, "Pot. Pretty high grade stuff. Guess they wanted to move it before it gets legalized."

He opened a black box and put a small bit on his tongue. "Cocaine. Damned well processed!"

The next box was the same. The third was pellets of crack. The fourth was heroine and the last "Some kind of designer crap."

"Well! About eight million bucks worth of stuff. How in hell could they move that much in a burg like this?"

Cummins said an hour or so later.

"Tranship. It's a tranny deal all the way through," The head team agent replied.

"Shit!" MG cried. "It was another type of tranny deal that got this mess started!

"I'm tired. I'm going home. See you Monday or sometime."

"We have to make statements and fill out a few hundred forms," Cummins replied,

"No. You do. I'll see you Monday or sometime."

That got him the bird, which he returned with a twist.

What a Weekend!

Sunday Blahs

MG woke up to another very bright day. That, by now, didn't hint at what the end of the day might be.

He had the car back, so he could go somewhere. He'd fixed everything around the apartment that needed fixing and caught up with e-mail and forums. Facebook groups had come to the point he could go on or off once a month or once a day and couldn't tell the difference on the debate sites. Apparently, no one bothered to look up the word and they all turned into nasty little bitch squabbles after a short time. It seemed that people with nothing to say had to get on the sites to repeatedly demonstrate they had nothing to say.

The natural medicinals sites were pretty good if they kept to the subject, but it was hard to not notice that people who were not Vegans or antacidists or one-plant-cures-all nuts dominated certain groups. It seemed that, if a person posted a number of perfectly reasonable arguments that disagreed with a certain POV of moderators they suddenly weren't there anymore.

MG had experience with that kind of thing. He was on a medicinal cure group, had done a lot of research to present, had hundreds of "likes" and "shares," then was suddenly banned from the group. He found the reason the head of the group gave to be ridiculous.

He then remembered the name of the moderator who posted a really radical way-out thing that didn't make sense on another group that was more about politics. He had made a reply that the post was poorly thought out, that it didn't take but one factor into consideration, and that consideration was unworkable if two other points were brought out.

That moderator had suddenly blocked him from the site, then he was booted.

A pity. That site probably did help a lot of people, but it also spread a lot of shaky information. At least, he had never posted anything on it that wasn't pretty deeply researched.

He had a suspicion about the head of the group, too. He suspected the group was financed by a big drug company to see that certain things that would cut into their obscene profits didn't go anywhere. Every suggestion about information by that head and the moderator led to sites that advertised products of the drug companies.

DUH! He had posted several things about the cheap natural cure that had worked for him, that he recommended for trials, that was getting positive reports, that he had written about and had posted it on the site, had included links to research reports – and it was used as a "reason" to remove everything he had posted because it was "advertising" – which really needed a convoluted justification, seeing the moderators' links were to blatant advertising sites.

So. He was coming up with a lot of hidden connections on the net because of a weird experience with a drug distribution scheme, even though it was very different types of drugs ... wasn't it?

The big drug corporations were keeping more people sick than they were curing. Even the cures depended on continuing to use products from those companies.

He had corresponded with a couple of scientists at major research universities to find they knew about his cure, but it was from a natural plant and wasn't patentable, which meant it could badly hurt the profit margin of the pharmaceutical giants, so publishing about it would mean funding of research would suddenly stop. It was that simple.

We live in one sick, sick world.

There was a knock on the door. He yelled, "It's open! Come on in!" before he thought. It could be that Nancy Ann silly teenage girl who kept flirting with him. She wouldn't take the hint that he was *not* interested in sixteen year old girls.

It was worse.

"I feel honored by being invited into the home of a lost brother! May the Lord bless you, no matter how you don't deserve it!" the preacher from yesterday's bus intoned. "I wish to discuss the many steps down the path to doom you have taken, and to make an attempt to help you find the true path to glory!"

Oh, pigshit! "Well, I do have a minute or two. I've spent the whole morning on the net, downloading porno, but it gets so boring after awhile. Same things over and over, just with different actors. A couple are real turn-ons, but you know it's all staged.

"Care for a beer? It's a little early, but it is Sunday, and it's five o'clock somewhere."

He felt evil. He would have a little fun.

"A *beer*!? ALCOHOL!? You offer *alcohol* to me, a man of God?"

"Why not? The Bible says moderation, not abstinence. It's hot, and a cold beer is certainly not immoderation, Sunday or any other day. Didn't Jesus, himself, give wine to people?"

"Er, well, that is certainly true, though the wine the Lord gave was not fermented."

"Yes it was. It was shown the word for grape juice was not the word in the Bible. It was the word for wine.

"I'm called MG. You are?"

"Er, uh, well, perhaps one. It is, as you said, not immoderation. Just one, that is. It is hot, and the Lord did supply ... a cold beer might be just the thing.

"I'm Ernest. My name. Ernest Gilliam."

MG got two beers from the 'Fridge and handed one to Ernest. He flopped down on the sofa and waved at the overstuffed chair. Ernest sat.

"You weren't really ... I mean, porn? You don't really watch that disgusting stuff, do you?"

"Not much. You run across it on the web. Somebody mentioned a site where gay Latinos were featured. I was curious. I expected it to be disgusting, but it was just the same as the regular porn. Some was disgusting and some was just people having fun. To each his own."

"I have never in my twenty seven years watched any of that stuff, except for a couple of things we found on a teenager's computer. The parents called me for help in saving their daughter. She was just curious, but she did no wrong. There is prohibition from doing those things, not from seeing pictures of them.

"I have never seen a gay video, though I admit to some curiosity. I don't really know what two men would do ... well, I've heard. Who hasn't?

"Surely no one would do those things on videos! Do they just hint or what?"

MG shrugged. The computer was sitting right there. He went to type in "gay X videos" in the search bar. A lot of sites, according to the notation at the bottom, 1,618,497 sites found. MG pointed to that.

"My dear Lord! *Million*! My dear Lord!"

MG went to a site that listed free gay xxx videos. The page came up, with about sixty photos of various acts. He noted that Ernest's eyes were weirdly bright.

"Let's see. Tags." He went there. "Hmm. blowjob, ass fuck, sixty nine, big dick, muscles, gloryhole ... what?"

"Sixty nine! Sixty ... I am somewhat slightly curious about ... I have heard of such a thing." He downed the beer. MG pointed to the 'Fridge. Ernest got another and popped it to sit staring at the screen, which had the sixty photos of men.

"Er, that fourth one on the second row! *That* is one of my own ... I mean, the one looks familiar, as though I may have seen him somewhere."

MG clicked on it. It loaded. Ernest was almost drooling.

"We really shouldn't be looking at this ... stuff, but looking at it is not against ... I mean, a person should have some concept of what a thing is if he is to explain the ... that is. Not do it."

"The new testament doesn't even say that. It only says not to fuck any woman but your wife. Not a word about gay shit. Christ lived in a time when gay shit was part of the society, even. I would think there would be a very clear prohibition, stated definitely, about this kind of thing if there was any prohibition."

"Yes! Yes! That is true, and it is the New Testament we serve. The Old Testament is history lessons. It is mostly just parables and wide views of what happened expressed as stories that are meant to be explanations of unknown things, is my theory. It was never meant to be taken literally.

"Have you ever done any of that?" He pointed to the screen, where the two were kissing and petting.

"Hmm. Yeah, some. It's not my thing, but it isn't unpleasant. If it's your thing, go for it!"

"Yes. I see. Gene is actually *very* handsome, isn't he?"

"If you say so. Who the hell is Gene?"

"He is one of my parishioners. I never *dreamed* he was gay!

"I have never dared even wonder about me doing anything like that. It isn't disgusting, is it? I mean, in that sense. It is just two people enjoying a sort ... sexual communication.

"*God*, he's beautiful! And so innocent!"

"Uh-huh. Ready for another beer?"

"Please! Er, may I use your rest room?"

MG pointed to the door next to the bedroom. Ernest went in and locked the door. MG didn't bother to get the beer.

Ernest came out after about six or seven minutes. He looked sheepish. MG got the beer and sat to bring up a group sex video. Everybody was doing everything. After about five minutes, Ernest said, "I'm still horny. I don't believe it. I have never done anything like any of that. It has me wondering.

"You say you've done it?"

"Some of it. It's not my thing."

"Er. Perhaps I should not be ... that is.

"Honest! I want to try it! You won't?"

"No."

"I wish I knew where ... that is, er ... fuck!"

"The one you said was in your church. Gene, was it? I've seen him around. He lives over on eighth, close to

Wildwood Street. He goes to that bar, I think. The Pink Rabbit."

"Er, are you suggesting...? I mean ... should I?"

"You aren't getting any younger. Life is passing you by."

"Yes! You're right! I will go there. It is true, the Bible does not say ... perhaps, because it is Sunday ... no. I never believed that anything is only wrong on one day of the week. That is misinterpretation.

"I thank you for the beer and conversation. You have opened my eyes. I was acting in a way I was told was correct, but it is not true. I have seen instances where the overzealous made strict rules they said were from the Scriptures, but they are not. It is from personal reasons.

"I will leave you. I think you are a friend."

"Yeah. Okay."

Ernest left. MG turned off the computer. That really wasn't anything that appealed to him, he had just seen signs from Ernest. Like he stared at any crotch that went by.

What the hell. Why deny what you feel? Why try to hide it? Ernest lived in a self-made hell because he tried to fight what was, basically, him.

MG didn't know if there was anything in the new testament about homosexuality. He'd never heard of it. Apparently, neither had Ernest. MG didn't care to read the Bible. It was boring and poorly written.

Weird world. Maybe his evil would be good for Ernest.

Somebody else came to the door. This time, he didn't yell for them to come in. Once was enough for one day.

It was Cummins. He said he just brought over the statement. MG could read it over and sign it or change whatever wasn't correct. He had a beer while MG read the four page statement. He shrugged and signed it.

"Got a bonus. Charlie was being intimidated and blackmailed by the one a step higher than the Cutters. We got him with his hands in the pot – pun intended.

"Donny is so spaced on crack he can't hold a thought, so we can't act on a lot of what he said. We can keep an eye on a couple more people."

"Do you always spy on my computer or is it only since this crap?"

Cummins roared with laughter. "You're not fooled for one second by this, are you?"

"I have gay porn on for a guest. You come here with a statement that could be signed Monday or next month or never. DUH!"

"Yeah. That stuff's not in your history much. A couple of things, but not the gay bit. Anyone I know who's in the closet?"

"It's none of your business. I wouldn't tell you if there was, but no. A preacher who couldn't look at a guy unless he first looked at his crotch. I gave him a couple of beers and turned that shit on. It turned him on. One of his parishioners was in a video. He went to look him up."

"Which parishioner?"

"You can – and do – watch all those things on the net and already know whatever there is to know."

"Fair enough. We'll watch the ones you showed."

"It's not any of your business. Get the fuck out of people's bedrooms. You're overstepping your authority."

"Maybe I just want to know for personal reasons?"

MG gave him the bird. He laughed. They chatted for awhile, then Cummins left.

MG turned on the comp, read the two e-mails, deleted

the forty six spams, then went to Facebook. Nothing that interested him much on the home page. He went to the groups. The medical ones, he answered a couple of posts about his cure discovery, then went to the Creaevolutsci Symposium.

The first two were exactly the same as when he went there last. Two sides, neither one of whom would give an inch, though the creationists didn't have an answer to give. It reminded him of an incident in a parking lot. Come to think of it, the next thread was the same and even included a sort of parallel to what happened after that.

Funny how closely life mimics life.

What to do? This was boring.

Maybe he'd go to the Pink Rabbit to see how Ernest was doing.

Nah! He was probably at his break-out orgy by now. There was nothing for him at a gay bar.

Well, maybe out to the lake. There were some pretty cool chicks there, and Sunday was a day late for much action. He was thwarted from any action by events, so could probably do well enough.

Nice to know your life has meaning and that you are accomplishing something.

He went out to get into his car. The next door neighbor had a car parked blocking his drive, which didn't mean anything, seeing he didn't have a car. MG listened for a minute.

"... you jerkoff idiot! What if there's an emergency and the ambulance can't get out?! What then, asshole!?"

"They ain't no amblance in thar to haf to get out, you stupid dickhead!"

"But what if there was?"

"If'n thar was, wouldn't be parked hyar."

"You stupid half-brained moron! You refuse to think about anything but your own convenience! Fuck head!"

"If'n you had un idee yur hed'd explode."

"LISTEN TO ME! IT ISN'T LEGAL TO BLOCK MY DRIVE! You have SHIT for BRAINS!"

"Well'n yur dun't got even thet."

MG was sure he'd turned the comp off.

C. D. Moulton's works are available on most major outlets as printed or e-books. CD writes the CD Grimes, PI mysteries, the Det. Lt. Nick Storie mysteries, the Clint Faraday mysteries, the Flight of the Maita science fiction series, books on orchid culture and many others of many types. Mystery, adventure, intrigue, science fiction, fantasy, paranormal, mild erotica, and factual.